This book is dedicated to all of those who needlessly suffer the indignity of living life without a solid roof over their heads and nutritious food in their stomachs.

To Wendy, who has put up with me for so many years, God only, knows how!

To all of my real friends. You know who you are and I appreciate every single one of you.

And finally, to my English High school teacher, whose name escapes me, you told me when I was 16 years old that I couldn't write, couldn't spell and never made any grammatical sense. You were right!!

Cardboard City

Alan Zoltie Publishing inc.
ISBN: 978-1-7374122-4-3

Who am I?

First off, I'm a guy who lived for a week as a homeless person on the streets of San Francisco. But who cares?

Yes, I did so, on purpose, and for no other reason than it intrigued me. I'd decided to write a book on homelessness in America some years prior to walking these dangerous streets alone and without money, a phone, or anything else the normal world entails. I'd worked with homeless people, either directly, or in homeless shelters, for many years, writing about them in my poetry and sometimes sitting for hours chatting to them in the streets or at dinner in the shelters, and figured the only way I could make my book come to life and be realistic, was to be homeless and experience the pain that is homelessness.

It was 2006, and I was 47 years old, and had been reasonably successful in my life choices. As a native of Great Britain, I had always believed that homelessness was one of the greatest humanitarian injustices on this planet. I found it hard to believe that with the resources the Western world had, that anyone, anyone at all, could end up homeless. It's been the bane of my life ever since, knowing that people, men women and sadly even children are walking the streets of America, without hope. I can't stand it.

I wanted to know more about homelessness, but how can you really know something until you've experienced it? I'm a man with deep passions and I crave a raw connection with reality. To me, life is the ultimate reality show. So finally, bored with business deals and having taken complete leave of my senses, I decided that I would live for one week as a homeless person.

I took the train to San Francisco, a journey of about an hour from where I lived at the time. Other than taking train fare, I brought no money. I had no cell phone. Nothing. I was ready to be set loose on those mean streets, begging for money, and "sleeping rough" as they call it in my native country. I didn't tell anyone what I was doing, because I knew they'd try to talk me out of it, and I might have listened. I didn't want to listen. I wanted to immerse myself in what it was like to be one of our society's forgotten.

It was one of the most frightening things I have ever done. I almost died on a couple of occasions. It was hard to sleep because I was always worried that I was about to be assaulted. Violence on these streets, as I was about to learn, is appalling. To eat, I had to beg for money. That was hard because of course, I was a complete fraud. I had plenty of money. It was horribly difficult to allow myself to go hungry because at any moment, I knew I could call one of my friends living in the city and within a short period of time, I would be rescued, showered, warm and safe, with a glass of Napa Valley cabernet in my hand and a good meal in my belly.

But I persisted, and I discovered early on, that passersby loved my Scottish accent. I was able to assert myself, along with my brogue, and because I stood out from the other street folk, I was then able to panhandle with some ease. I suspect it was obvious to people that I hadn't been on the streets that long, hadn't had my spirit beaten to a bloody pulp by that grim, endless cycle of shelters, crime, desperation, hunger and brutality. I looked hopeful, and I was.

To make money each day, and pay for food, most of which was fast food, I'd walk up to someone/anyone, mainly visitors to the city and ask, "Can I help you with your tourist needs for five dollars?" Some people were charmed and said yes. Most walked away with a look of disdain and horror. "Where are you from and how did you end up here?" being the most popular question I was asked, after I'd introduced myself. To some, I was honest, telling them what and why I was doing this for, but for others, the majority, I just took my money or my rebuttal and moved on, never knowing if any of them even looked back with a second glace to see if I was going to be OK or not.

After one week, one very long week, I returned home. What did I learn? I learned that there are a lot of good souls on these vicious streets and an equal number of bastards. I learned that it takes time to figure out who you can trust. I learned that there are a few people on San Francisco's streets who are in their seventies, have been homeless for years, and thrive on it. Some of them, con artists, going home each evening to a house they actually owned! Some raking in $40,000 or $50,000 a year, tax-free. I didn't care for them, because they were taking resources away from the people who really needed them, genuine homeless ladies and gentlemen, who didn't have a warm bed to go to at night, who had no regular income and who only had scraps they scavenged to feed off. Most of all though, I learned that I really didn't ever want to be homeless again.

And then, a few years later, I sat down and put this book together in the hope that I could raise funds from its proceeds for some of the charities who support our homeless population and who try endlessly to put an end to one of life's greatest injustices, living each day without a roof over one's head and inspire more people to get involved in an effort to try to rid our streets of these homeless souls.

As a native son of Glasgow, Scotland, where I inherited what can only be described as a disarming sense of humor. I was born on the two hundredth anniversary of the birth of the poet Robert Burns, close to very town where the author of *Tam o' Shanter* came into this world, January 25, 1759. Whether because of some mystical Burnsian connection or just my upbringing, I tend to see the funny side of even the worst situations.

My father and grandfather always taught me to respect every person that I met in life, no matter what their profession or standing. They believed, quite rightly, that the only reason you are where you are in life is because of where your mother happened to have sex with your father. The intrepid little sperm that became me could have just as easily gestated into a Darfur refugee camp or a repressed North Korean hostel. But thank goodness, neither was the case, and simple old Glasgow, Scotland was my given destiny.

It lends one a little perspective, not to mention gratitude.

I'm also a serial entrepreneur. In high school, I failed an important exam and doomed my chances for university. I wasn't terribly upset; formal education wasn't really my cup of tea. But my father was concerned. He asked me what I was going to do with my life. I told him I was going to sell plastic shopping bags. Another of my father's favorite sayings was, "It doesn't matter how you make a living as long as you make a living." I think my choice of vocation tested that philosophy...that is, until the head of Scotland's Indian Mafia gave me an order for 10,000 plastic shopping bags to use in his take-out food service restaurant.

Yes, you read that correctly. *Scotland. Indian Mafia.* I was standing on Gibson Street in Glasgow, where most of the city's curry houses were situated at that time, and the *capo di tutti capi* of said criminal organization told me he was going to introduce me to every Indian restaurant in Britain and make me rich. And damned if he didn't do it!

He also made sure that for the next two years, I ate free at any Indian restaurant in the United Kingdom. To this day, when I perspire, I think it still smells faintly of masala sauce. But my career as an entrepreneur had begun with a bang. In 45 years, I have never worked for anyone but myself.

From those early days as Scotland's plastic bag baron, it was on to licensed promotional products, advertising on golf course benches, pins with artwork of famous athletes on them and many other novelties that made me a comfortable living. Eventually, I could be found commuting between the U.K. and San Francisco every few weeks (a punishing routine I kept up for eight crazy years) and designing jewelry for some of the world's biggest brands: Nike, Coach and Victoria's Secret, to name a few.

Along the way, I burned through a marriage or two, and basically paid the price for my decades of nonstop traveling, brand building and deal making. Which leads me to the third of my multiple personalities, after voluntary vagrant and lifelong businessman.

I'm also a poet.

Given that this is a book of poems, perhaps that's obvious. I've written more than 400 poems about the homeless and another 4000 plus on other subjects near and dear to my heart. Perhaps, in this book, Cardboard City, I'm cleansing my bloodstream, though my writing, of what I saw during my week living on the streets of San Francisco? I'm an accidental poet, finding time to write despite the fact that everyone I knew told me I had no literary talent whatsoever. Damn the torpedoes; I wasn't about to let a little thing like a complete lack of writing experience or training stop me!

When I discovered my talent, or lack of talent, I wrote and I wrote, eventually writing books that have been published and in their own way, that have also been successful. In a feverish two weeks, several years back, (bringing to mind the breakneck pace with which Jack Kerouac wrote *On the Road*) I finished a novel about a man and woman who meet on prom night, become collaborators in a terrible crime and wind up working for competing companies in Silicon Valley. Later I wrote a nonfiction book about one of the companies I'd been involved with, and the experience of elation and then disaster, as that company went bust. Neither book has been published and probably never will be, but that's hardly the point. My forays into the territory of the dependent clause and subjunctive case were for myself, to salve my soul and limber up my libido, or some such nonsense.

So it was that on my birthday in 2003 I found myself in the impossibly picturesque and romantic town of Half Moon Bay, California, on the coast about 90 minutes south of San Francisco. Things were not going well; I was having a fight with my wife and wondering what direction my life was to take next. As I sat on a rock watching the waves conclude their long trek across the Pacific by dashing themselves to spray upon the beach, a poem came into my head. Such a thing had never happened to me before, so I wasn't sure what to make of it. Little did I know that this was one of those seemingly inconsequential moments that pivot life in an unforeseen direction.

I wrote the poem down. Why not? Later, I sent it to Paul Trevillion, a great friend and partner in crime who just happens to be an extremely successful artist in England. Paul was neck-deep in his own depressive gray cloud at the time, but when he read my poem he phoned and said, "This is brilliant. How the hell did you do that?" I honestly didn't know. I certainly had no confidence that I could do it again, but at Paul's urging. I submitted my humble verse for publication in an upcoming book of poems.

It was several months before I heard back from the book's publisher, and during that time, it was as if someone had opened up a sluice in my subconscious. I couldn't stop writing poetry. It was a compulsion. Obsessive rhyming disorder. By the time the publisher called me, I had written 40 or 50 more poems on the subjects I knew best: sex, drugs, rock and roll, babies and dogs. Wonder of wonders, not only did the publishers want to print my Half Moon Bay poem, but they wanted more! I wound up getting fourteen pages of verse in that book.

With that encouragement, the game was afoot. I became a poetry machine, Robert Frost on steroids. Since 2003 I've written more than 4,500 poems. I write at least one a day. Some are fit only for a class on how NOT to write poetry, but so what? I never set out to impress anyone with my skills. I've always specialized in pentameter for an audience of one.

Still, I wanted to share my passion. I started a website dedicated to my poetry, www.alanzoltie.com. I began writing poems about autistic children and sending them to the Autism Society. Some of those pieces wound up being read by more than 350,000 people in Britain. I started playing up my Burns connection and people started suggesting, "Is this the reincarnation of Bobby Burns?" This was both utterly absurd and ridiculously flattering. I was having more fun than I'd had in years. I felt impassioned and recharged.

That is the path by which the book you're holding came to be. It came about because, as I hope you have discovered, I'm a man of deep feelings for life. I love dogs. I feel pain for the homeless. I think life should be simpler for all of us; it's too complicated now. I have no idea whether I'm a personification of Robert Burns or a cheap knockoff, but I know I don't want to die and be a stone in the ground. I want to touch people. This collection of poems is a part of that. I hope some of them touch you and bring to you a bit of the passion I brought to creating them.

I know this: life is sliding doors. My father (who was quite the one for pithy aphorisms) once said to me, "If you were standing up to your neck in shit, and someone threw a brick at you, they'd miss." Translation: I'm a lucky man.

Lucky enough to have a chance to share a little bit of what sparks my soul with you. Damned lucky is right.

Alan Zoltie
2022, Laguna Beach California.
www.alanzoltie.com

Foreword

I'm often asked why? Why homelessness? What was it that drew me in, that made me want to get involved, that ignited a spark inside my mind imploring me to act against homelessness, one of mankind's biggest travesties? When exactly did I figure out that this would be my calling, writing a book describing not only my own experience, but bringing to the forefront of public attention what it's like to live as a homeless person? All of these legitimate questions rang through my head for years, and then, quite by chance, I remembered!

It was the summer of 1973; I was 14 and living in Glasgow Scotland. It had been a cool day; normal by Scottish standards where 65* is positively balmy, when the doorbell at our home suddenly rang. My mother was cooking, my two sisters were fighting with one another as per usual, and so that left yours truly to go and open our front door. There, stood a man, completely unknown to me, half chewing a piece of cake, some of which was sticking to the inside of his mouth and the rest, quite noticeably the outside. He had on a grey trench coat, a well-worn trilby hat and wore at least three to four days of grayish white stubble. He reeked of body odor, although at the time, and being only 14, I just thought it was an unhealthy smell coming from somewhere outside in our garden, which just happened to make its way inside when I'd opened the front door. He was trying hard to talk, his four or five missing teeth quite evident as his mouth began to open, when suddenly my mother's arm came swiftly over the top of my head as she took command and bumped me into the background of what was about to become, a heated, one-way, conversation. I sensed her anger as she pulled me behind her, her words flowing, and they weren't kind.

"What do you want?" she shouted at the unknown gent standing on top of our doorstep. She said it in such a condescending ruthless manner that I was completely taken aback. My mother was never obnoxious or rude to anyone, but I knew immediately something was really bothering her, as she launched a verbal tirade at this poor man.

"What is it?" her voice was growing louder and even more angry.

"Can you give me something to eat?" He asked, quite politely, I thought.

"There's a place where people like you can go!" She was shouting once again.

'People like him?' I had no idea who he was, but I sensed my mother did.

"Who is he?" I asked her time and time again. I didn't like her tone or the way she was speaking to him. I recall being quite upset as my mother had always taught me to treat people as I wished to be treated myself. I stood there silently, witnessing her bombardment at this poor man with such a powerful verbal onslaught, it left him looking even more distressed than he'd been when I'd opened the door to him. My mother suddenly slammed our front door shut, disgust and fury written all over her very red irate face.

Giving her a moment to calm herself, I asked, "Who was that?"

"A schnorer" she barked. (A schnorer in Yiddush is someone who asks continually for hand outs and wants nothing more than to feed off those who work hard while doing nothing constructive to improve their own situation and standing). Probably 'beggar' is a better explanation.

"He was Jewish?" I asked, flabbergasted that my mother would turn a fellow Jew away. After all, wasn't it a mitzvah (blessing) to help those who weren't as well off as we were? We'd always been taught that Tzdakah (charity) starts at home.

"He can go to Copland Road. They'll help him there" She shouted angrily with a dismissive wave of her hand. She was mad. I couldn't remember ever seeing her in such a menacing state.

Copeland Road was the Jewish center in Glasgow. They held dinners, dances and special events for the Jewish community in Glasgow and also prepared kosher meals for the elderly and infirmed and delivered them too. This hall was approximately 6 miles from our home.

"But that's a long way from here" I pleaded.

"Doesn't matter. He needs to bother them, not us. That's why they are there, to help people like him" she scowled.

And there ended our conversation. She retreated back towards her kitchen, her mind steaming with rage at the insubordination shown by a fellow Jew.

It took me another year or so to come to terms with the fact that the man with whom my mother had spoken that day was actually homeless. In Glasgow there were only 6000 Jews, and to find out that one, perhaps more, might be without a home was staggering to me. All my friends came from decent backgrounds and upbringings; in fact, I didn't know anyone who had a parent who was jobless, let alone without a roof over their heads. We all seemed to survive, albeit with some struggle and with some dissatisfaction of one kind or another, but homeless Jews?? No way! It just never happened. We looked after one another. It was an unwritten rule. How wrong I was.

The feeling of helplessness my mother's attitude towards that homeless Jew had left inside my head, rankled inside me for years. I knew then, that both of us should have behaved differently. We should have fed him. We could have done so without much difficulty or hardship. It would have been easy to give him a sandwich or piece of meat. Truth be told, it would have been easier than losing face and boiling up a rage by refusing to assist.

In my head I was a humanitarian, although I didn't have any idea what a humanitarian was when I was 14. In my head I was annoyed with my mother, but I didn't know why I should be because she was older and wiser than I was. In my head I was confused, but in my heart, I was saddened that any human being, Jewish or not, had to go door to door to beg for food. It just made no sense to my naïveté. Perhaps it was my naïveté that made no sense? Whatever it was, I was sure there was a solution to make not only my mother calm down, but to make it possible for that man or any homeless person to eat without the indignity of having to ask for handouts.

THAT is when I realized I needed to try to do something about a situation that affected millions. That day, without realizing it, changed my life. I knew I had to at least try to change the lives of the many who found themselves in the same place as that man did. To try to help change as many lives as possible, a task that would prove significant and almost impossible but a task all the same. And never being one to shirk a challenge, here it is, Cardboard City.

Cardboard City is a book that I hope will help raise not only money for those who find themselves living homeless across this planet, but also bring a greater awareness to this despicable cause we all seem to believe can just be swept under the carpet by being generous with our donated dollars. Cardboard City contains extracts from my own experience of being homeless for a week in San Francisco, a week that was often harrowing, frightening, death defying and, to say the least, monumental. An experience which left an indelible mark on my soul and gave me the opportunity to experience first hand just how incredibly sad and uncaring we have become as human beings.

From the Embarcadero to the district South of Market, my journey started and ended with nothing other than respect and genuine sadness for most of those who find themselves homeless each day, and with total disgust for those who are using and abusing the system for their own short-term gain.

In Cardboard City I have compiled many poems based on characters, good and bad, with whom I had the opportunity to observe, chat with first hand or just pass by. I hope these poems will give you all an insight into what it's like being homeless in San Francisco, New York or any other place on earth.

I lived in London for 14 years, after moving from Scotland when I was 18. My office was situated, close to Regents Park Zoo, and in that particular area homelessness seemed to be rampant. There were so many homeless people running around one of London's most affluent suburbs, that it seemed to be of epidemic proportions. It was hard to avoid making contact with these people, because there were so many of them living in this one place. I used to talk to some of them on my frequent trips to the underground train station (read Tube) at Camden Town. It was incredible! Some were war Vets, some runaways from all towns North of London, some were addicts and some just liked being homeless. Yes, they liked it! But they were few and far between. The crux of the matter was, there were hundreds of them, just in this one locality, and many thousands, just like them spread all over the capital city. Money it seemed wasn't the solution, nor was food. The solution so I discovered, lay not with the government, not with people like you and I and not with society itself. The answer could be found inside the hearts and minds of those who were suffering this indignity, this incredulous situation that left tens of thousands of men women and children without a roof over their heads, and the rest of the country, or world, with all it's resources, technologies and wealth, ignoring, to the most part, their plight. Human beings! They just wanted to be treated as such, and not pariahs or outcasts. Give them their dignity, give them real life and opportunity and perhaps, just maybe, they would give back.

All very simple, all very possible, but sadly though, all totally ignored.

In the USA alone there are nearly 2.5 million homeless people and from that figure, over 150,000 are children. And that's just the one's we know about. It's believed there could be as many as 1 million more and that the average age of the homeless in the USA is a staggering 9 years old! In Santa Clara County where I resided for 20 years, they try to account for all the people who might be homeless by sending out groups of volunteers each night. These brave souls go where you and I would never walk, their main aim, to carry out a daily census of sorts and to try to obtain accurate figures of those who are seeking shelter and then house them. Several organizations subscribe to the thought that we can end homelessness with just a little bit of creativity, beginning of course with government intervention. Although the chances of this ever happening seem to be slim to zero. We all live in hope that one day, and one day in the not too distant future, a solution might be found that will at least take those who would like to be housed, off cold uninviting streets from where they reside and into affordable safe housing. Remembering the old adage, if you don't have an address, you can't get a job, if you don't have a job.....

There is an unused talent pool out there. Amongst depths of depravation there might lie many who could or would contribute to our society, as shown in several documented cases from the past twenty years. Famous and not so famous people who, with not only luck but determination, have pulled themselves out of that cesspool of desperation and made their lives and the lives of others not only more tolerable but also unbelievably whole.

With Cardboard City I would like to sell one copy for every homeless person in America today. All the proceeds from my book will go to shelters around the country, programs that assist the homeless and some with the direct intent of aiding people I have met who need just a little kick start to get their lives back in order. When I began my crusade, I had no idea I was even riding towards this goal, but now that I've arrived, I feel blessed and honored to have been apart of something that could perhaps be life changing. I cannot do it all myself, none of us can, and with a little help from you, all of you, I can assure you that together, the start we could make to eradicate homelessness from our country would be welcomed and remembered throughout communities, cities and states for decades to come. One small step could make one huge dent in one of today's major issues.

God Bless and thanks for your support. If you would like to email me, I am always open to conversation and to comment.

- Alan

Desperation and Depravation

How would I describe depravity? Would my description stem from personal experiences gained from traveling around the USA, or from traveling to another country and witnessing first hand the total injustice that life can bring for so many unfortunates? Would my perceptions come from the heart or just from within a thought or ideal? How could it be that so many human beings don't have the basics to live a normal healthy life? What we fortunate's would describe as our recognized existence?

And what about desperation? Can desperation be seen through the eyes of the unfortunate, even when they smile? Of course, to live in desperation encompasses more than just a need for all of the simple things it takes to survive each day. Desperation can also be found in war torn environments, countries engulfed by famine, and even countries that are living in relative peace. Desperation is many things, unfortunately too many to count, but when considering its meaning, one needs look no further than our on our own doorstep. Look outside, and on every street corner and you will see them, homeless people, men, women and children alike. There are over 2.5 million humans living this way and more than 15% of those who do, are children. The average age of a homeless person in the USA is a staggering 9 years old, and yes, you can see them everywhere.

Desperation and depravity means sleeping each night on a concrete slab, being unable to wash, eat, poop or act like a civilized human being. It means being cast aside as an unwanted animal, which unfortunately sums up the demographic in most homeless people in America are placed.

To observe, is not to partake, and although observation can be a great leveler, it pails into comparison with the reality of living through that experience first hand. When all worldly possessions are cast aside, when there is nothing, including and especially, dignity. When being ignored, beaten, spoken to like the trash you have become is commonplace and expected. This is desperation. This is depravity, and I lived it. I lived it for one week, probably the worst week I have ever lived, but I did it. I experienced first hand what it is like to live on cold wet streets with nothing. No money, no friends, no place to sleep and no way out, which is what I promised myself I would stick to no matter how difficult, how rough and how scary life became. I dedicated 7 days, really not a very long time in anyone's book, to experience what I believe is one of our nation's great injustices, to let any human being live without a roof over their heads and without food in their bellies. To let our streets become home for those who are unfortunate enough to end up there, without caring deeply enough to end their misery and along with it, the guilt of our own misjudgment.

1

Life is harsh, life is cruel, but life is here for living. We, as humans, are only here on this planet but one time, so with all that said, in my humble opinion, we are here, as human beings, to live life and to assist those who need help. We are here to make life more comfortable for those less fortunate than ourselves. We are placed on earth to give as much as we can give, and most of all, we are here, but for the grace of God.

When you read the following pages, please bear in mind that I knew I could leave and go home at any time. I wasn't stuck there, and I do appreciate that I was doing this by choice and not because, like the other 2.5 million homeless people in America, because I had to. I could just walk away and rejoin society as I'd left it, with my car, my home and my huge comfortable bed. But I didn't. I decided that I had to be an unfortunate, no matter how false that situation seemed, and believe me, there were times when going home would have been so easy and made much more sense than sticking to my original plan of one week and no less. I did not embark on this experience to receive plaudits, to be congratulated or to relieve any guilt I had inside my own mind. I did this because I wanted to, I needed to and I sincerely believed that once my journey was complete, I could write this book with some authority, and justification. I had spent years observing homelessness from a distance, but this was an opportunity that would be unsurpassed, just trying to survive as they do, from day to day, or really hour to hour, and often minute to minute. I take my hat off to all of them, and I shed a tear for those who try, really try to get out of this chasm that seemingly has no end. There are some who need to be homeless, some who pretend to be homeless, but mostly there are just those who are stuck being homeless, and it's to them that I go to bed each night reciting my prayers to a God who I often don't think exists, but someplace in my heart keeps me hoping that one day life will be shared equally by every one of his flock. That day, as of today, is one day closer, and with the purchase of this book, your money will be placed directly in the path of those who walk these streets every day with a fear that this day would never arrive.

When you read this book, when you delve deep into the lives of people you'll never see, never meet, never want to be, understand that these people are not fictional characters and although I might have changed their names, and perhaps some of their descriptions, they do exist and as far as I know, they are all still living in the squalor and loneliness that is desperation and depravity. Remember also, most of them never believed they would end up this way and more importantly, most believe they can ever get out.

And So It Began

I had a stash, but just how I'd accumulated this crap was beyond thinking about. My issue now, while the evening was young, was to find a hiding place for all my 'goodies'. As dusk began to fall over San Francisco, my second afternoon had been filled with fear, curiosity and trepidation, although my first day had been worse by a country mile.

I seemed to have found an excellent hiding place behind a portable toilet, just off the Embarcadero, underneath the Bay Bridge, hidden from everyone's sight other than the few who already used it. But to me, it seemed deserted, with the chance of anyone discovering it, in my opinion, minimal. It wasn't a resting place for me personally, only for my stash. My stash included, a section of solid brown cardboard slats, a light grey 'painters' sheet, two empty plastic bottles, an old toothbrush, a couple of tin cans, again, both empty, a roll of toilet paper and a pen, all accumulated during a march through the city with some other 'friends' the night before. I'd also managed to scrounge some plastic bags to make life easier when it came to carrying my 'gear' around town. My clothing consisted of a dark blue coat, circa 1970, three sweaters, all with holes, all unwashed, a tee-shirt, newish, only because it was an undergarment and no one could see it, underwear, just like that tee shirt, fairly new, a pair of pants that were too big for me and which were held on to my waist by some string and a little duct tape, and shoes but no socks, that I'd retrieved from a Goodwill stand before leaving for the city. I also had a scarf, more like half a scarf, and some torn gloves, which I kept in one of my coat pockets. My money, the money I'd managed to collect so far, was safely tucked away, or so I believed, in one shoe heel, which, just by good fortune, was loose and spun in and out around 90 degrees, creating a cavern suitable to hide dollar bills but not loose change. I was dressed to kill, dressed to kill time, the most sensible and economical way anyone who is homeless can possibly dress. This was San Francisco and this was not going to be pretty. I was shit scared, had very little money, and no food. I had no place to shelter, no real friends and no way out. I was in for the long run, a week (a small sacrifice for someone just pretending to fit in), which is what I'd promised myself I would do, and there was no way on earth that I was giving up before that week was over.

Previous Afternoon-Day 1, Arrival

I'd arrived in San Francisco penniless, a deliberate ploy. I'd taken enough money to hop on a train from San Jose, (about 55 miles south of the city), leaving all my worldly possessions and comforts at home. I'd told no one, not even family or my business partners where I was going, and now, having just stepped off a

BART train at Embarcadero station in the middle of San Francisco's downtown area, (it was 4 30 PM and I was hungry), frightened, confused and undecided whether I should go straight back home to my warm comfortable king-sized bed, or, just plod around the streets for one night to see what might happen. The emotional drain that this decision had placed on my weary mind was to say the least, exhausting. It would have been very easy even without money to skip the barrier at that station and head straight home to a warm bed, food, and all the other things that we normal people expect and take for granted. On the other hand, how was I supposed to write my book about homelessness in America if I, Alan Zoltie, had never experienced what it was actually like to live on these streets where survival is key? With my courage kind of intact, and putting on a 'pretend' brave face, I headed towards Fisherman's Wharf where at least I knew there would be lots of people hanging out, those sharing my plight as homeless and those who were not. With a little luck and some guile, I thought, just perhaps I might be able to assimilate with those who were homeless and feed off those who would probably look down on me as a nuisance, a vagabond, a panhandler and scum of the earth. This was my new life, my chosen life, but for most, this was real life and a way of life I was about to hopefully embrace, if only for a short period of time. My nerve ends were tingling and I desperately needed to take a crap. Now, under normal circumstances, I would have just walked into the nearest hotel without even giving it a second thought, found a bathroom and taken care of my business. Not now! I had no idea what was supposed to happen, and within minutes of leaving that station my task of surviving without anything other than my cunning and wit had really begun. Without a place to take a crap, in my mind, this experience I'd so carefully planned, might end just as quickly as it had begun!

The Embarcadero parallels a busy sidewalk, which then parallels the San Francisco Bay. There are normally so many tourists and locals using this path for walking, jogging, skateboarding and sightseeing, that sometimes, depending on the time of day, it can be hectic to the point of distraction and very difficult to navigate. It's hard to avoid this onslaught of humanity at the best of times, but when you are a homeless person that no one cares about, no one will give you a second glance and most people avoid you like you're the plague. Which, by the way, with so many homeless people around, plague is not a word that should be used lightly. It made for a very interesting first observation. Instead of crowds of people just brushing past me as they normally would, they seemed to just give me a wide berth trying hard to look away trying hard not to notice me and trying even harder to make sure they got past me without my asking them for cash. Total avoidance! I suppose in a city that's filled with over 40,000 homeless people, everyone else becomes accustomed to seeing outstretched hands and arms looking for handouts. I couldn't blame them, and I had acted in very much the same manner for many years when I'd driven up from San Jose to spend a day as a tourist or visitor. I was instantly struck by the manner in which I'd become a leper. I must have exuded that frightening glow, you know the one that every homeless person has, dressed in old smelly clothing, unshaven, no possessions, and a glassy-eyed stare that says 'feed me please'! I had to get to a bathroom and was on the verge of crapping my pants when suddenly and without warning; I was tapped on my shoulder from behind. I was startled, and immediately frozen to the spot. I slowly moved my head to the right and behind only to see an enormously fat lady, dressed all in pink, about 5 feet tall, with no shoes, and a hat the size of a beach umbrella, looking up at me. She must have weighed 250 lbs., at least!

"What do you want?" I asked, talking down to her as if she was insignificant.

"You're not from this section?" she said

"What section?"

"This one. What you doing here?" she asked

"What do you mean, what am I doing here? I need a crap. Where do I take a crap?'

She was obviously a panhandler, and homeless, but this was my chance to get started and to hopefully gain some valuable insight on how to survive the night.

"You need a crap? How much you got on you baby?"

"Nothing, I just got here" I replied

She studied me in an interesting way. Her nose had begun to twitch, just like a dog, a kind of sniffing action from left to right. She then looked me over from top to bottom. It felt like I was her master, ready to bark out a 'sit!' command. She was making sure I was safe, making sure I was friendly and checking my credentials without uttering a single word. When she finished, she began talking again, her nose now in a resting position.

"Follow me" It was a command.

"Why?" I asked. But before I had a chance to repeat my question, she was off. There seemed to be no second chances here, and following my gut, I decided this lady could be the only lead I would get that night, a lead that could lead to a meal ticket and a crap and therefore pursuit seemed to be my best option. She was quick, shrewd and obviously extremely street savvy. She was marching at the speed of her two short legs towards who knows where, but I knew that if I didn't go with her, I would probably crap my pants before getting the chance to find a place to do it legally and safely, and there was no way I wanted to spend my first night in jail, although the thought of doing so was tempting only from the standpoint of getting a bed and a meal and someone to chat with. No wonder our system is so fucked up!

Have you even thought about what it would be like to be rejected by all of society just because of the way you looked and the situation and circumstance in which you found yourself? Down on your luck, no money, no home, no food, no respect? Well put all of these together, and that's what being homeless feels like. You are hated, disrespected, trodden upon and mistreated by everyone, including innocent little kids, yes children! People despise you. Well, most people do. They know you have nothing and they just ignore you, they won't look at you and they often refuse to come within 10 feet of where you stand. It's incredible how things change when you have nothing, when you are smelly, dirty and penniless.

Pinky, which is what we will call her, led me to the back of a fast-food stall near Pier 39. She suddenly stopped, looked at me, and once again began that sniffing motion with her nose. Up, down, left and right. It was hilarious, and disconcerting.

She very quietly said to me,

"Go in there, take a dump, and do your best not to make a mess"

I looked, hesitated and made a move to open a wooden door. The door had a padlock which had been broken. Inside, the stench was unbelievable. Somewhere between stale urine, shit and rotting food. I closed the door, sat, released my bowls and automatically looked for paper to wipe my bum. Of course, silly me, there was none! I really didn't know what to do, other than put my pants back on and walk out. I was disgusted, screwing up my face into a knotted wrinkled ball as my underwear touched my dirty skin, but this was my life now and there was no way out other than going home to San Jose. I opened the door and exited back into the daylight, but by then 'Pinky' had vanished. Gone! What was I supposed to do now? It felt good that my bathroom experience had gone down without a hitch, other than the lack of soft paper to wipe up, but now I needed food and a place to stay and some money and I needed to find some toilet paper and a few other incidentals that I knew I would need to survive the week. I wasn't sure where to start, but I made my way up to Fisherman's wharf sat on the cornerstone of a monument and thought about my next move. It was obvious to me from what I'd seen over the years that a blanket would be a great addition, some cardboard to make a shelter, and anything else I could find to make things more comfortable during these next 7 days living on the wild streets of San Francisco.

One thing that kept entering my mind while I sat on that stone watching seagulls and listening to the sea lions performing their theme songs on the wooden floats that had become their second homes, was that if I was hungry and if I couldn't beg for food, then with some cash, I'd be fine. I only needed $1 plus the tax, to get anything off the $1 menu at McDonald's, and unlike a lot of the other homeless people who seemed to be mulling around I didn't have an alcohol problem, drug issue or a need to blow my cash on cigarettes. Every penny I could make would go towards food. With all that said, I was very nervous about even trying to beg for money. I had never done that before, and one cannot just stick out a hand and say 'lend me a dollar pal'. It doesn't work like that. It takes courage and a certain amount of chutzpah! I had to continually rehearse what I was going to say. I was about to take other people's hard-earned cash, and if I was being totally honest with myself, it was just as easy for me to go home not take their money and feel good as it was to be sitting here contemplating hunger and the thought of continual rebuke from those who passed me by 'loaded' with cash! And if they did pass me down a bill or two, then what? Would I get served at Micky D's, or would they treat me like the dirty, smelly, unwanted mess I really was? There was only one way to find out. Try it!

"Can I borrow a dollar pal?" My first attempt, said in a broad Glaswegian accent, and sounding pathetically quiet and subdued. My hand outstretched, my head bowed, my heart pumping blood towards my shaking legs and sweaty palms. Sweat also rolled down the back of my neck from fear. My eyes looking forward yet never making contact with anyone, searching for anything other than their frightened or disgruntled faces. My determination to succeed, non-existent!

"Can you please spare some change?" this time louder, more assertive just like I'd seen the 'pro's' doing. I was getting the hang of this! The hang of what, you might ask? Well, the hang of taking money that was hard earned for most, and using it to satisfy my own survival and curiosity. What makes people give to other people? What was the incentive for anyone to give to any homeless person, a person they'd never met, never known and probably would never see again? I for one always looked at shoes. I figured if they didn't have decent shoes then things must be really bad. So, why would anyone give to me? I had to have a hook, a draw, a reason. That reason would then give me a distinct advantage over anyone else who was begging in my vicinity. My smile? My hair? My accent? I just needed one hit, that way I would figure it out, and build upon my good fortune, just like I'd done in the past with my regular life.

"Please spare a dollar for a homeless Scotsman!" I was now very assertive with my tone and with my demeanor. I even smiled a little, hoping this would work.

"Where are you from Pal?" His accent quite recognizable, his face completely unknown to me.

"Same place as you" I replied.

"What happened to you?" He was reaching into his pocket to retrieve what I believed to be a dollar bill. His wife, or girl friend, was standing next to him quietly embarrassed and pulling at his coat sleeve in a manner that suggested she would rather not be standing there witnessing the conversation that her beau was having with a smelly homeless person.

I wanted to be upfront and tell him that I was doing research for a book and that there was nothing wrong with me and that nothing untoward had happened to me, but I stopped short of doing so and went into an unrehearsed diatribe about how I had come from Scotland to make money in the computer industry, lost my job, lost my money, lost my home and then lost all sense of belonging. He stood there silently eyeing me up and down, undecided if I was telling the truth or not and trying hard to determine if I was just another junkie or alcoholic looking to make money to take another hit of my favorite beverage or white powder. I could tell he was totally flummoxed and confused. I spoke quietly and with my usual smile, so I knew I was unlike all the rest of the homeless tribe he'd already encountered during his stay here in San Francisco. He was obviously intrigued because he continued.

"Any idea what direction Ghirardelli's is?" he asked.

"Yep, it's about 3/4 of a mile up that way" I said, as I pointed him in the right direction, "And their ice cream is brilliant! Have a fudge sundae if you can, you won't be disappointed. When you're done there, I would suggest One Market St for dinner"

He looked at me like I was daft (Scottish slang for stupid), and the confusion spreading across his face was there for all to see. I knew he was trying hard to figure out in his own mind how I could possibly know these things. It was obvious to me that he was trying to compute 2 and 2, but was only arriving at 3.

"Any other places you can suggest?" He said, as he raised his eyebrows in a way that suggested I was perhaps a fake, a plant and that there was a TV crew just around the corner filming his reaction for one of those 'America's Funniest" shows we watch regularly on TV.

I proceeded to give him a very long list of places to go. His wife/girlfriend, now a little more comfortable with the situation perhaps knowing that I wasn't going to mug them, wrote down every word I said on a sheet of paper she'd mustered up from her Coach handbag. It turned out that not only were they from Glasgow, they were from a place three miles from where I was born. Small world. We concluded our 'tourist' information conversation, and without warning, he pulled out a $10 bill and handed it to me.

"Make sure you get something to eat with that son?" he said, and as quickly as he'd come, he was gone. I'd done it!! I could now not only eat; I could also get the train home if needed. I was elated, yet sad, but I accepted that I'd passed my first test and then realized how, going forward into the week, I could easily make more money. Tourism!! That was the key my to success. In the meantime, hunger had struck a nerve in my head and a chord in my stomach, and I decided it was time to find out if I'd be served at the local McDonald's, located just a few steps around the corner. After I'd eaten, I thought, 'I'll begin my search for some 'necessities'.'

Tourists, and a few locals, formed a straight line in front of three cash registers. And then there was me. Everyone who'd watched me walk in looked like they'd just seen the first coming of an alien or the resurrection of Christ. They instantly tried to avoid me, taking one step either left or right and trying hard not to brush against my shabby clothing or look me straight in the eyes. I could tell that they were all talking about me. I knew I didn't smell that bad, after all this was only day one of seven, but their obvious perception of who I was supposed to be and what I represented was there for all to see. There had been many times in my past, and I could recall nearly all of them, when I would go into a fast-food restaurant and see a homeless man or woman in a corner with nothing but an empty cup. I would always, without exception, offer to buy them food. My thought process was that I was better off feeding their hunger by buying them whatever they wanted, rather than feeding any bad habits they might have just by giving them cash. At least I could see them eat and not squander any money I would give on drugs or alcohol. I presumed, wrongly of course, that some nice person might have the same opinion of me, as I stood in line alone waiting to be served. No one offered me anything other than avoidance.

"Please can I have a number 1?" I asked politely.

"Got money to pay for that" the young lady asked from the other side of the counter. I took out my $10 and handed it over. She double checked it, just in case it was a forgery, put it in her cash register and gave me the change. I, just for the sake of pissing her off, triple checked the change, just in case she thought she could stiff me. That made her scowl even harder. She went away, and within 10 seconds, returned to the counter, threw my meal down and with a gruff, "thank you' and a forward nod of her head, wished me a 'fuck off out of here' goodbye! I would not starve tonight! I sat in a corner, stared down by all and sundry. It was unnerving. I savored the taste of this junk food as if it might be my last meal for a while, thinking aimlessly about what it would be like to do this every day in life. I couldn't fathom how people did that, how they went from one day to another without the continuity of a regular income, a home, a family, friends, and all the other things I just took for granted. At that particular moment, I felt extremely alone and sickened by the thought of all the others out there who had absolutely nothing. My heart just sank and my appetite vanished. Suddenly realizing that my day was nowhere near being over, I jumped out of my comatose state with a jerk! "Where was I going to sleep?" It was now just after 7 PM, and it would be dark in about 30 minutes. I knew there were shelters for homeless people in the city, but how did one find them and how did you get a bed? I would have to find out, and find out sooner rather than later. I gobbled down the remains of my dinner, finished my drink and before I set off in search of a place to stay for the night, I went to the bathroom to steal some toilet paper for future use. Armed with more than half a roll that I'd managed to unravel through a 'locked toilet roll dispenser, I came out of McDonalds, proud that I'd passed step one in my adventure, but that's when everything started to become difficult and my worst nightmares began.

McStarving

McStarving sat, with her large sign, larger belly and even larger dog
Begging for McNuggets, outside, in the summer's heat
Putting on a show for all who believe in fairytales
Looking sad, then happy, then even happier, as her dog was offered a McBone

Impossible, sang those who rushed by, with more important chores to finish
Majority decision, though some kindly stopped and thought
Second chance in the center of a huge McFlurry of people
Leaving a dollar bill by the side of her chutzpah

And then, the sign changed, she was now homeless and in need of beer
A more honest approach for the remainder of this passing crowd
Finding instant success in the form of a half-finished McBeer
Guzzled quickly, and then passed on to her now thirsty mutt for completion

Three hours later, and yet another sign, McStarving and McAddict
All of a sudden, a multi tasker, looking for a serious McJob
Given donations, by a now seriously annoyed and sullen fan base
Returning from a McBeating by relieving their McConscious on a McFake

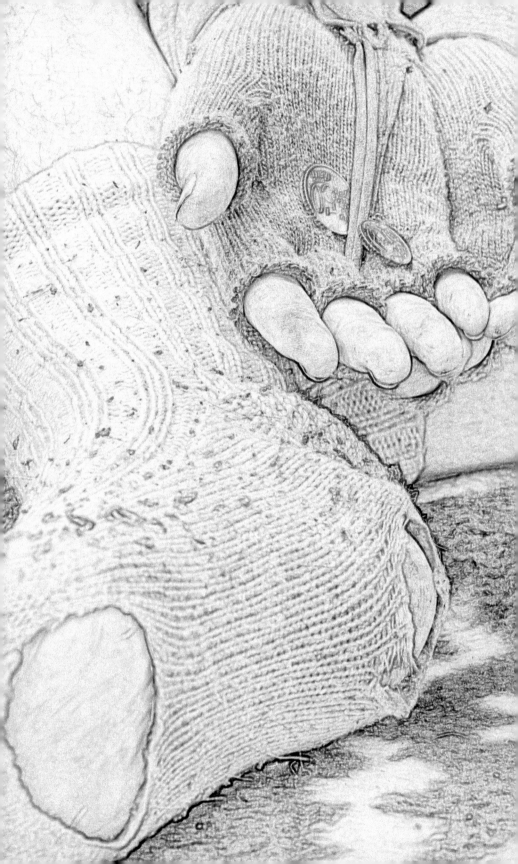

At the east end of Market St where The Embarcadero and tram lines cross, and the BART Station intersects with the ferry building, there are many homeless men and women who hang out, hopeful to receive hand outs from passers by who might care to give. Most pass without even looking them in the eye, but now and again, and more often than not an 'out of towner' will stop, stare and be 'conned' into passing over a buck or two in the hope that the ugly dirty face in front of them will just vanish from whence it came without creating an embarrassing scene. It's often surprising to see an educated homeless person being shunned in favor of one who is obviously crass and far from being polite. I can never understand why the fear factor of looking into a dirty face outweighs the need to give to a clean face? Perhaps it is just that simple, the fear? The fear that if a dollar isn't forthcoming, that dirty face will get in *your* face and make life unpleasant. Looks however aren't everything, as I was about to find out.

Although dressed up like a homeless person, my face was clean, if slightly unshaven. My attitude however, was totally different from most of the other homeless people who frequented Market St at Embarcadero. I was polite to perhaps the point of being too nice. It was, after all, the end of my first day in this city posing as a homeless vagrant. I believed I'd done a great job up to this point; however, I was still a virgin when it came to being homeless at night-time and believe me night-time was horror time and nothing at all like day time. As the streetlights came on the sun went down, and dark shadows turned into black and grey silhouettes of the city landscape, every idiot known to mankind, every vagrant, every druggie and everyone in need of their fix, violence, alcohol, sex, and all things seedy and disgusting, arrived. As if by magic, to commence yet another evening of illicit criminal and gang related participation, they all appeared out of nowhere. It was incredible! These so-called human beings just appeared! It was as if the gutters in the streets had opened and every rat that had ever set foot on concrete emerged. Some hungry, others, starving, but most were just looking for a place to bed down for the night or a place to stop and practice whatever perversion, addiction or illusion, they were going to perform until that warm orange sun rose again the following morning. It was frightening, and it was frightening within moments of sunset. It didn't happen over a period of let's say, an hour. No, it happened all at once, just like birds stop singing as nighttime falls, and sudden silence engulfs one's tuned in ear. This was madness. From all over, bodies, more than I could count, sprung out of nowhere in particular, all ready to fight like dogs, for scraps, scraps that were indeed, extremely limited.

As I sat back on my perch the top step of which surrounded a WWII monument, I was aware that things were going to be tough, certainly tough for someone like me, someone without a clue on how to survive this carnage of humanity. And yet, all around, life went on as if nothing was happening. It was about 9 PM, and tourists were touring, locals were relocating and people were just really going about their lives as you or I would have had we been in such a place at this particular time. Restaurants were filled, theaters were emptying, bars were crowded, and yet, here I was, here we all were, homeless, with nothing to do and no place to hide. It looked like we had all become a huge unwanted wart in the middle of the city of San Francisco waiting for someone to come along and clean us all up. Only that never happened, and after several minutes, which seemed like hours, watching all of this unfold my priority of course was directed to finding shelter or indeed something that could act as shelter. I knew I could manage without food until the following morning, goodness me, I thought, 'I have fasted for 25 hours many times before', for religious reasons, so a few hours in San Francisco should be easy. I also knew that if I could find food, or was offered food, like a squirrel saving up for winter, I would take it and keep it for emergency purposes. But shelter was a priority. Where to start?? Did I need a blanket? Could I find a shelter? If I couldn't, where would I rest my head for the night? Should I walk, should I run, should I stand and hope? All these thoughts and more were running through my mind.

In San Francisco, there are many hostels for the homeless, some of which I'd read about before leaving the comforts of my previous life, which now seemed like weeks ago even though it had been less than 24 hours. The only thing I remembered, and which really stuck in my head like a bad nightmare, was that if you didn't manage to get in line for these shelters between 4 and 5 PM each day, you were screwed. There were so many homeless people in this city that the shelters couldn't cope. If you were one of the lucky ones, and you did indeed find your way into that 'lucky' line by 4 PM, not only would you get a bed, sometimes and by chance, you could get a meal, and often a shower. But unfortunately my luck was not to prevail on this particular evening, my very first evening of being homeless, and I had already missed my opportunity to bed down inside the 'luxury' of one of those aforementioned city dwellings. I knew that if this particular night ended up in disaster without finding shelter, then tomorrow, I would be on my way to stand in line by 2pm and not 5pm as was always suggested! For now though I needed assistance but was unable to fathom which homeless person I could talk to, never mind trust. My first attempt at communicating with an unknown, ended up in a slagging match.

"Yo!" I said nonchalantly, to this 'tramp like' figure standing just a few feet from where I was perched. "Where do I go to get a bed?"

"Fuck you asshole" came his curt response. "Go wherever the fuck you want white boy" and he started to walk towards me with a menacing strut in his drunken or drugged up two-step. 'Fuck' I thought, and decided quickly to move, and move like the wind. There seemed no point in getting myself into trouble this early in my stay, and really, what chance did I have against a seasoned veteran of these mean streets? He could've been carrying any kind of weapon, any kind of disease and any kind of grudge, so a left turn and quick step towards a more secluded part of this section of town was required, post haste! My retreat was brief. Before I knew what was happening, there were at least 5 other bodies blocking my path to freedom. My new best friend in life had called in reinforcements. Where they had come from? I had no idea; all I knew was I was surrounded and about to become chicken feed for this madding crowd. I decided to take the bull by the horns and go on the offensive. In my broad Glaswegian accent, I blurted out loud.

"You fuckers want to take on one of the Queen's guards?" To this day, I have no idea what possessed me to say that, but it stopped them all dead in their tracks, totally bemused, dumbfounded and unable to continue on their path, a path, which I presumed, meant beating the shit out of my fragile being. So, there we all were, in a stand off of sorts, just like a Clint Eastwood spaghetti western. Them, surrounding me, and me, with bravado now my only friend, about to embark on a Scottish tirade of foul and abusive language in the hope that I could cuss better than them, and that my profanity would be enough to ensure they knew I wouldn't be a pushover should a fight ensue. I was shit scared, shaking like a leaf, and about to pee my own pants when, without me really knowing why, my voice took over, and I began to scream.

"You stupid Yankee fuckers! Come any closer, I will knock seven bells of shit out of all of you, AND, I will take great pride in doing so, for the Commonwealth, for The Queen, and most of all for the great country of Scotland!" Silence. They stopped. They didn't know what to do. I didn't know what to do! I had them flummoxed, and all of their evil intentions seemed to just evaporate. My words had been brief, but effective. They backed off, at least most of them did, but, as is often the case, there is always one who has to go that extra mile, that half yard further, that one step closer, just to see, just to be sure and just to prove a point. And, here he came. His long black coat looked menacing enough, never mind that 'kill' tattoo wrapped around his neck. He was coming closer and closer and then, without notice, other than his ugly face and bad breath, he was on top of me with his hand wrapped round my throat.

"Tonight, my friend, you die" was all he could say.

Looking at him, trying hard to breathe, I smiled, as best I could, and in a very quiet voice, I spoke these immortal words. "I do?" He looked at me, and laughed, then let go, and stood up looking down at my body, which by now was squirming with fear. "No, you don't" And just like that, he offered his hand in friendship and elevated me back up to a standing position as if nothing had ever happened. What the fuck was going on?

"Never seen you here before my friend?" Geez! Now I was his friend? I was so confused, but I ceased on this opportunity, this break in violent proceedings, to get comfortable in my new skin and befriend, what I hoped would be my ticket to a good night's sleep.

"Alan" I said, as my hand was outstretched looking for natural reciprocation. He just looked back, never offering anything other than all of the mistrust that was written right across his beaten face. He was obviously the leader of this 'pack', but right now his voice was bathed in silence as he tried hard to sum up exactly who I was and why I was standing here in front of them so obviously a complete contrast to anything they were used to. His mind was working hard and I could see that his inability to decipher exactly what my intentions seemed to be left him dumbfounded and confused. "Why you here?" he asked, talking in a language without verbs.

"Same reason you are, I need a place to stay, I have no money, no food, no friends, and no hope" They laughed.

"No, why you in this country?" He wasn't smiling.

"I got lost on the ocean, and was washed up in that bay!" I said, as I pointed to the water at the end of the street. Sarcasm seemed to be working, and suddenly some of his cohorts were laughing.

"Scottish?"

"Yep, that's what I said" hoping now that being a 'foreigner' amongst them would have its advantages. They looked at one another, and then at their leader, the one who'd flattened me, and it seemed they were deciding whether to invite me into their little 'gang' for the evening.

"Got any money?"

"Nope." I lied

"Food?"

'Nope" I shook my head, knowing it to be the truth.

"Fuck" he was pissed. "Weed?" he was getting more pissed by the second. "Pills?" I shook my head in the negative. "OK" he said, "Come with us. It's time to scavenge" And with that last statement echoing across Market St, his whole crew including me got up and started to march, like an army unit, but without weapons, food and direction. I failed to see the purpose of this little adventure. Right then I was tired, lonely, scared, and although intrigued, I could sense that this was just the beginning of what would become one of the longest nights of my entire life. But for now, I was content to join this madding crowd, in the hope of a bed, some food and perhaps, and I use this word lightly, some friendship.

No Name

No name, no identity, no longer wanted
No place to go, no inspiration, no hope
No food, no smile, no chance
No idea what happened, no way to return
No friends, no good Samaritans
No life

Sitting amongst affluence, unable to touch
Watching closely as the past repeats itself
Placing a stolen mind inside the pleasure of another
Dreaming casually of what used to be
Remembering with some disdain those pitfalls
Realizing the cruelty of his downfall

No salvation, no direction, no possessions
No welcome, no love, no adulation
No feelings, no spirit, no self confidence
No pleasure, no fight, no happiness
No comfort, no recognition
No end in sight

Unbeknownst to many people who frequent San Francisco on a regular basis, and unbeknownst to me too, there is a geographical fact about the city that is quite staggering. There are 43 hills that make up the city, and it was built on every single one of them. This makes it very tiring to walk, unless you are super fit. The hills of San Francisco rise way up into the sky, well, it seems that way when you're at the bottom and you need to get to the top. I was with my new friends, a gang of sorts, and it had become our mission to walk across town from the Embarcadero to the Mission, at least that was the plan being communicated down through the ranks, and since I had no choice no experience certainly no will to be on my own, that was the plan I was prepared to follow. Our gang consisted of 11 people. 3 black males, 4 white, 1 Hispanic and 3 white women, all of who had seen better days. When I finally came to my senses after being grabbed unceremoniously around my throat, I began to converse with some of these homeless souls who'd once had lives similar to what most people would call, normal. Each and every one of them had stories to tell, as I would find out over the next few days, but for now the only one who intrigued me was Oleg. Oleg was huge, probably 6'6", 240 lbs, and had the reddest hair I'd ever seen. His accent was Eastern European although not Russian, even though his name suggested that he could hail from that particular country. Oleg's beard ran about 8 inches off his chin, having not shaved for at least two years. His hair was long, way down past his shoulders and his skin grey and wrinkled from exposure to the elements. His looks and build suggested he was around my age, maybe 50, but when I began to 'interview' him, I was shocked to learn he was only 29. He dressed in anything he could get his hands on, and on this particular night, the night he'd grabbed me by the throat, he was wearing a grey/green coat, unbuttoned, because there were NO buttons placed where buttons should be, and three sweaters, all different colors, one on top of the other. His pants were black, and his second-hand Nike's were ripped from top to bottom. He was not a picture of perfection, but in a strange way, he was smart, and he was so obviously proud of his dress sense. A homeless fashionista of sorts! Oleg had a black backpack, which was filled with the great unknown, and only Oleg knew exactly what was making that backpack so obviously heavy. He never shared; neither did any of the others. Law of the jungle, rule of thumb, and possession is 9/10 of the law. That's just the way it was out there. No one ever questioned anyone else's bounty or swag, and no one ever stole from anyone else. If they did, the consequences were dire, as I would find out in due course.

"So, Oleg, where you from, originally?" I asked. Now that a channel of communication had been opened between us, he was more inclined to speak to me candidly, since he knew I posed no immediate threat.

"Poland" he replied, "but my family brought me here when I was 14"

"You still have an accent then?"

"Yes, it helps to keep the fucking American's scared" came his response. He had such a Slavic tone in his voice and his words were spoken in such a deep guttural manner, that I could understand how people who didn't know him might be frightened in his presence. He was, after all, a huge man.

"How did you get into the state you are in, sorry, WE are all in, right now?" And so, Oleg began to talk as we walked, a walk that would take at least an hour, relating to me in very descriptive language, stories of the abuse that his drunken father bestowed upon his slight teenage body when they moved from Warsaw to LA, and how each and every scar, both mental and physical, had driven him into this wanton desire to leave and make his own way in life. This is the brief version, but the real version was epic, and probably worthy of a Hollywood blockbuster movie! Oleg had wandered on his own from the age of 17, up to Northern CA, arriving in San Francisco when he was 22. He had been without a home for most of the 12 years since he'd left his parents care, obtaining the odd job here and there and even making enough money at one point to afford a room rental close to a job he kept for a year in Santa Barbara CA. With everything that had gone on in his past, the abuse, the beatings, the uncertainties, Oleg never found it possible to maintain an even keel in life or to spread roots whenever roots appeared to be growing. Oleg eventually gave in and decided, this was it, his destiny was to remain homeless, his future, like the rest of these homeless people, was always to remain uncertain and irrelevant to any who looked at them from the 'outside'. A blight on a normal landscape, as he always reminded me. "I see my task to survive, but my road is blocked by others who see me as nothing but a parasite, a worthless piece of shit, someone who means nothing in society, and I have become what they all believe," he paused, 'I have become nothing."

His last statement was a fact and resonated endlessly amongst all of the homeless people I was about to meet. Through no fault of their own, and I know a lot of you out there will completely disagree with me, they have become nobodies, worthless, inconsequential and a sight for sore eyes that we all just wish to ignore in the hope that they will just somehow vanish. This is really not the case. When speaking to Oleg, for the first time, but not the last, I had my eyes opened. Oleg was as much a human being as I was, and if not for abuse, bad fortune and an inability to integrate into 'normal' society because of the way that society is perceived, Oleg was as capable of living as good life as anyone else on this planet. Only Oleg had not had the opportunities afforded to the majority of us who take for granted our every day comforts. And, there was more to come, more that I hadn't bargained for which took me completely by surprise.

"How about you?"

"What about me?" I responded, in a rather surprised manner. We were still walking to our final destination, wherever that was going to be, and now, I found myself at the other end of a barrage of questions I hadn't planned for, nor had I ever thought of preparing answers to. I presumed that I would come to San Francisco, walk these streets alone for just a week and never meet anyone, let alone ever talk to anyone. I was there to observe, not to interview or be interviewed. Oleg's questions arrived completely out of left field. It hit me straight in the center of 'oh shit, what do I say now?' I thought about it for a split second and decided to go with the truth, well it was a half truth, but close enough to be acceptable and plausible at the same time.

"I had no place left to go. My heart wasn't in the life I had and I wanted to get away from all the grief that was surrounded me, so, without any ties, no home, no work, no place to go, I ended up here, with you guys, and to be very honest, this is my first night on the streets, here in San Francisco!"

"First night? You're VERY first night?"

"Well, eh, no, not exactly" I was backtracking now. "It's my first night in THIS city"

"Ohhhhhhh!" And by now all my new friends seemed to be nodding at the same time. I had won them over and as suddenly as they'd started, the questions ceased.

I discovered early on with most of the homeless people who have experienced many years of 'street life', that simple answers often suffice in taming curiosity. I believe that this comes from an ingrown fear, the least they divulge about themselves, the better, just incase it shows weakness. After all this was the jungle. Conditions most of these people were living under, and fear of being overpowered or bullied could come from any kind of weakness, verbal, mental or physical. Most street people tended to keep their mouths shut and get on with their daily tasks of finding food and shelter. Keep it simple, because life had become too complicated and led them all down this path to loneliness, destitution and irrelevance.

The hour was late, way past my normal bedtime, but yet, I felt wide-awake and totally at ease with the circumstances which surrounded me. Having Oleg and his chums as company obviously helped, but in general, my life was now completely different. Without a timetable and no particular place to go, why get uptight about stupid things, like going to bed early in order to rise and do emails, workout and eat? I wasn't able to do any of these so-called 'normal' things, and so my immediate thoughts were guided towards each footstep I was now taking into that great unknown. And great it turned out to be.

Territorial

Two days, two trips, two different directions
Marching on his beat
Staying clear of direct contact
Knowing his place
Territorial for sure, soaking wet for certain

Not once but twice
He remained as was
Looking for what appeared to be nothing in particular
A route march towards nowhere
Comfortable in only his stride pattern

Bed, tucked under a withered right arm
Face, black as the night he feared
Beard, unshaven for many years
Clothes, old as the streets he now walked
Smile, nonexistent, but determination to survive, unbreakable

Vanishing in moments behind another tree
Lost amongst bushes, now his home
Leaving no trace and no requests
Gone, until fate determined his purpose
Reappearing tomorrow in the opposite direction

Sleepless In a Gutter

Have you ever slept in a gutter, or ever imagined sleeping in one? Have you thought about sleeping on a park bench, by the side of a road, any road? Have you ever slept on a street corner with busses, cars, trucks and humans traipsing past you right through the night without a moments respite? I have and it sucks. But I only did it for a short time, my friends, Oleg and his crew, had to do it every night and after following them all over the city that first evening before settling down somewhere close to Golden Gate Park, I formed a new respect for their plight, a respect that only accelerated my intention to make this book happen.

It's 5 miles to walk from Market St to Golden Gate Park but when you arrive at the park, and at that point I wasn't only hungry and thirsty, I was exhausted, you are introduced to a completely different section of homeless people from those found downtown. By different I mean they have a new set of priorities, only because they 'reside' far away from the famous and frequented tourist spots of San Francisco. Most of the people I met in this area were far calmer, far more reserved and far more laid back since they'd left the madness of the 'jungle' we'd just walked away from at the wharf. Their attitude to life on the streets was much more communal and spiritual. They had a will to survive as a team and not as individuals. They were, pleasant? Yes, that's it, pleasant in comparison to those who lived and stalked downtown San Francisco.

Oleg gave the order, "we will rest here" and just like that, in the pitch black of a wooded area inside Golden Gate Park, we stopped, sat and waited for his next command.

One of the ladies, Celia, was shaking. "You nervous, cold or desperate for a fix?" I asked her.

"I don't feel well, and I'm hungry" she replied.

My heart sank. If I was who I was supposed to be right now, my real self in my real life, I would have taken her home, bathed her and fed her and given her a bed to sleep on. Celia was a gem. She was 28, from Arizona, Tucson to be exact and had run away from her husband when he started beating her, just over two years ago. The promise of a fresh start, new friends, a new job and a new outlook on life brought her to San Francisco where she was unfortunate enough to become seriously ill just 4 months into her new career as a waitress at the Cheesecake Factory restaurant. Without insurance, without sick pay and without anyone to help her out, she lost her job, her will to survive and eventually her dignity as she eventually joined the swelling ranks of San Francisco's homeless population. Yes, from rags to rags, Celia's story had so many parallels with many of the other's I would meet and talk to. There always seemed to be some kind of life changing tragedy that had led to homelessness.

"Oleg" I shouted, "let's try and feed Celia, she's not doing to well"

"Listen Scotsman, I am in charge, I'll sort her out" he replied as he began to walk menacingly towards me. I wondered if my throat was about to feel the strength of his fingers once again?

Oleg stopped short of attacking me, placed his heavy backpack on the ground next to Celia, took out some bread and cheese and fed her.

"Where'd you get that?" I asked.

Silence.

I never asked again.

Within 20 minutes Celia was happy and the shaking had stopped. Oleg was off talking to some other people we'd stumbled upon who were also in the woods and ready to bed down for the night and the rest of our team or gang were quietly fixing themselves bedding from the blankets and other items of comfort they carried around in their bags or coat pockets. It was after midnight and it was cold, although not freezing. That famous San Francisco fog had engulfed the city and along with it, our 'team'. Oleg threw me a blanket, I lay it on the grass and within 20 minutes everyone was asleep, everyone except me.

As I looked around, trying hard to relax and perhaps get a few hours sleep on this anonymous grassy hill, I realized that most of these people had a 'stash', blanket, water bottles, extra clothing, little bits and pieces that to us, would mean nothing, but to them, meant life or death. I made my mind up that tomorrow, which really was today since it was after midnight, I would have to join in the scavenger hunt and equip myself. And with that in mind, the next thing I knew or felt was drizzle from that dense fog dripping slowly, endlessly, although gently onto my cold face as light began to surface from the east on this, my second day of being homeless in San Francisco.

Streets of San Francisco

I have walked this path a hundred times
Watching closely, looking sideways
Seeing only dregs of yesterday
Unable to come to terms with greed of today
Lost souls left lonely and sad
Bearing guilt that has now become immense
Treated only as pigs and rarely as men
Fallen heroes under lights that are now dimmed
Punched to the floor with complete indignity
Unwilling to forgive, never able to forget
Pawns, in a war of attrition
Used by politics as fodder for powerful games
Landmarks on the streets of San Francisco

Marched like penguins, all black and white
Waddling in line to an occasional oasis
Boasting endlessly about time spent alone
Sincere, but only when fed sufficient fuel
Fighting anguish amongst their demons of hope
Set loose to reconvene and reorganize
Shadowing possible care givers that rarely give
Isolated and berated, assisted by only the few
Dominating an already dominant sky line
Falling short of everyone's expectations
Recognized merely as pariahs
Fixtures, forever permanent
An embarrassment with an easy fix that can never vanish

Breakfast? There was no breakfast. Instead of a welcoming smell of coffee, fresh bread and or donuts, perhaps a rasher or two of bacon, some breakfast sausage and yes, of course, scrambled eggs, the only stench that would permeate my nostrils on that particular morning was weed, marijuana and cigarette smoke. It was disgustingly stomach churning and very unwanted. A quick and very stark reminder that life was back in gear for those who had so little and traveled so light. It always bothered me that these people had no place to live, nothing to eat but they all had cigarettes, drugs or alcohol. It made no sense, and I was determined to uncover the reasons why their addictions were endlessly fed, and more importantly, by whom were they being fed by?

Packing up as efficiently as possible, Oleg had made it clear we would all traipse back to the wharf that morning, another 5-mile hike, not something that would have bothered me on a full stomach, but having barely eaten anything other than a Big Mac in the past 24 hours, the thought of climbing those huge hills, just to return from whence we came, well, that wasn't on my agenda. I thought it might be better to hang around the park and build new friendships, in the hope that something or someone better than Oleg would enter my new and very strange existence. It was time for me to abandon my 'friends' and abandon them I did. Without warning, I went for a little walk deeper into the park, and I never came back. My itinerary was going to be self-serving, and to do so, I needed to break from the grasp of a Polish dictator and his flock. I'd decided that if by chance I met up with them again, I would just say that solitude was my passion and solitary excursions served my purpose better than group involvement. Something told me that I would never see any of them again, but one never knew. At that point in time, it was back to feeling hungry and with some of my cash, I had about $7.50 left, I was out in search of more fast food to quench my starving tummy.

It didn't take long to find a new bunch of homeless buddies willing to chat and share their stories. About an hour after feeding myself, again, breakfast sandwich and a bottle of water for a few bucks relieved my pain from fasting all night, I remained on the west side of town, where I thought the friendlier 'vagrants' would be found. I wasn't wrong, bumping into several men and women who were all too keen to reach out and explain their current circumstances. My accent of course was the ice-breaker, and as soon as most people hear me talk, they were almost always all ears and full of conversation. I, on the other hand, was keen to listen and not to talk, which I managed to do most of the time, and when required would add a few words here and there just to give my audience some piece of mind that indeed I had a voice and therefore a past. I knew that around mid-day I would need to begin my search for a bed for the night and also for supplies. I needed a blanket, some other, extra clothing, more money to buy food just in case I couldn't get into a shelter, and I needed a place to stash it all, because carrying all of the above would be nothing but a bind and I didn't have a back pack or other carrying receptacle to assist. Once I collected all of these items, I would have to hide them and then go back each night or afternoon to collect them. There was no way I was carrying them around all day. I'd decided simplicity, if possible, was my number one priority. After all, I only had 5 more days to go until I could go home, so why make life difficult? Right?

Golden Gate Park and its surroundings was so much more preferable to being at the wharf and downtown San Francisco, but honestly, the lack of possibilities due to the fact fewer tourists came into the park, made it difficult to panhandle and ply my new trade of being a tourist guru. I'd made a choice to follow Oleg and his gang, and now it was time to return to the city, hopefully in time to get a bed and to make some cash for more burgers and fry-up feasts. '5 miles back?', I thought, no problem. 2 hours max and a good healthy walk into the bargain. Off I went, head down, mind set and radar on, looking at every street corner for anything that I felt might come in useful if I had to spend another night out in the open air.

It wouldn't be long before my aimless collection began. My very first item, a lovely warm, and nearly clean, blanket. It was sitting on top of a bench at a bus stop. I thought, at first, that it must belong to someone, after all, there were four of five people waiting for the bus to take them to wherever they were going. They were all lined up and waiting to board as the bus pulled up, and as I cautiously examined each and every one of them, hoping that the blanket didn't get removed and my hopes dashed, after the last person paid his fare and the bus moved on to it's next stop, there it remained, all ready and waiting for Alan to come in and relieve it of its loneliness. What a find! One mile later, I found a few sheets of carboard that I could use as a bed. Half a mile after that, a dirty pair of socks, which I had no idea what to do with. My biggest issue remained, finding a way to carry all of my 'plunder'.

Plastic bags were aplenty, so why not grab a couple and fill them with the items I'd found? Of course, when you're a 'normal' person, getting bags is easy, in fact, there's a never-ending supply, and they are everywhere. When you're a homeless person however, the simplicity of such an easy task, grabbing an extra bag or two, becomes a nightmare scenario that takes some cunning and guile and a huge set of bollocks to boot. You would never think that plastic shopping bags meant so much to so many, bearing in mind they are given out with gay abandonment at every store in the world, creating the huge issue we have today, pollution and their inability to bio-degrade. Try walking into a store, any store, as a homeless intruder and asking, very politely, for a plastic bag! "Fuck off" "Fuck You" "Get out you scum"

Just some of the responses I received as I tried aimlessly for an hour or more to get my hands on just two plastic shopping bags. It brought me right back down to earth with a bump and gave me an instant realization that as a homeless man, albeit and intruder, no one wanted to help me with something as simple as giving me a stupid 1 cent plastic bag! I eventually found a bag in a garbage can that would suffice and as is always the case, about ten minutes after that, I was presented with dozens of bags, just lying in the street, untouched and ready for use. It's just like waiting for a bus. You wait hours, nothing happens, and then suddenly, three come at the same time, all going to the same place!

The thing that I thought about most that day, as I walked back across town, was how incredibly pariah -like I'd become, without any effort whatsoever. I'd been instantly compartmentalized by most of the general public into this seedy, unworthy, filthy, miss-represented character, who no one knew, but who everyone wanted to avoid. They made no bones about how they all felt, and unfortunately, this is part of the problem with our current society. Yes, there are bad people everywhere, but there are also good people, in every walk of life. Having worked in homeless shelters for many years, my philosophy was always, treat them as you would wish to be treated. Nicely, and with dignity! Something I have always believed in.

Box Of Tricks

Once filled and brimming with goodness
Emptied by need and so much regret
Lying opened and sad against a wall of little hope
Placed there by an unknown savior
Ready and waiting for permanent occupation

Each flap, slightly torn and soggy
Satisfying refuge for a man claiming membership to humanity
Pulled from street to street by chance
Arriving happily at this, his new front door
Cursing luck that had turned at the drop of a coin

Proudly dragging this box of tricks
A smile, showing blackened teeth, brimming with anticipation
Knowing wholeheartedly, he would sleep tonight
Covered by the emptiness of someone else's good fortune
A treasure amongst streets paved with only concrete

Into a distant corner alongside an open mind
Placing everything, including his soul, inside this new found crib
Resting, perhaps not entirely, into tomorrow
Thankful that this had been his best day in months
Amazed by how incredible an open carton could be

A quick digression from my escapades in San Francisco.

San Jose, The James F Boccardo shelter for homeless, Sept, 2010.

I arrived ready and willing to volunteer, something I'd done many times prior to that evening, although never at this particular shelter. My task, to help serve meals to over 200 residents and nonresidents, assisting the chef, Paul, his assistant Dawn and her other two volunteers in placing the precooked meals into large heated trays and assembling them, the meals, onto plates, enabling the residents to form a line, 25 at a time, get one piece of everything and then sit and enjoy their hot food in a proper dining area. In other words, let's try to make a relatively small number of homeless people feel welcomed and satisfied, and also make them feel like human beings. When I arrived, I was amazed to find some of the homeless crowd already in line, desperate to be first into the kitchen/dining area, which didn't open until 5 PM. It was 4.25.

I was fortunate to keep this volunteered position for over 5 years, something I really enjoyed doing, and something that in my own mind, gave me great internal peace, knowing I was doing my part, no matter that it was a very small part, in helping people who were completely down on their luck and not in any position to help themselves. However, on that very first evening, as the line started to form and the dining room doors opened for service, I was standing behind a glass screen putting green beans on to plates that already had other protein and carbohydrate elements placed on them by volunteers standing to my right, when I noticed a man coming into the room in a wheelchair. My eyes caught his struggle, an unfortunate victim of his own demise. He had two hands on his wheels, pushing as hard as he could, an dinner empty dinner plate on his knees, a cup wedged between his armpit and his body and the glasses on his face tilted to one side and about ready to fall off. I left my station, jogging towards this man, offering him table service, something I at least, believed he deserved.

"Just go to a table and I will bring you food" I told him, as he handed me his plate and cup. "Would you like ham or beef?

He was very kind and responsive with his reply, "Beef please sir!" he said, "and thank you very much for your kindness"

"Of course," I said, as I removed a chair from the table he was headed towards, leaving room for him to park his wheelchair.

When I jogged back to the counter, Dawn asked me

"What are you doing?"

"Helping that disabled guy" I replied, as I pointed towards the man in the wheelchair.

"We don't do that here" she said, and she said it in quite a condescending manner.

"What do you mean WE DON'T DO THAT?" I asked

"It's every man and woman for themselves here. No special service for anyone, not even the disabled"

"You are not being serious?" I bellowed. "We should treat everyone with respect and dignity, and the disabled are no exception" I was very annoyed, and Dawn, who was technically my boss, made it perfectly clear to me that if I did the same thing again, (there were many wheelchairs in that dining room on that particular evening), I would not be welcomed back.

I thought to myself, "fuck this and fuck her' and I decided to carry on offering table service to anyone who was wheelchair bound, in direct contempt for Dawn's orders. I didn't care if they never let me back in again, I was determined to make a difference, and a difference I made. All my efforts turned out to be worthwhile. After my standoff with Dawn that night, of course I was invited back, and as I said, I spent almost 5 years, once a week, performing the same voluntary work, until I moved away from that area. The following week, I saw the fruits of my labors come to life, when the wheelchair crowd, who'd not seen me for 7 days, made a point of applauding me after my second meal service, having all been given the same respect I gave them the week before. They felt like human beings and not the 'scourge of the earth' that so many of them believed they had become. This whole experience taught me many lessons, one of which, respect for fellow man, led me to my thoughts that day I was walking back across the city of San Francisco towards the wharf. What if everyone treated everyone else on the planet with respect and kindness instead of disdain and hatred because of their social standing or place in society? Wouldn't life be more tolerable for those less fortunate? Of course, it would, but it will never happen, at least not in my lifetime.

Skinny

She was thin
She was skinny
She was anorexic
She looked miserable
She had a child
She gave him food
She shed a tear
She made a call
She lost her temper
She went bright red
She fell on her knees
She pushed her baby
She wanted out
She cried once more
She couldn't hear
She was so pale
She was incapable
She was on drugs

As the fog rolled in again, I was close to the wharf area. It was around 4 PM and time to make some money. Firstly, though I had to hide my stash. I found this derelict building under the Bay Bridge, right behind a porta potty. It was a chance I had to take, leaving everything in one spot in the hope no one found it and stole my 'entire life' and more importantly, my nighttime protective gear. Thinking about it now, how stupid was I? Well, I didn't know any better, so what the heck? I left it all there, nicely camouflaged with some trash that was also lying around, and I headed off to find some cash and a bed for the night. The thing was, which should I do first? I decided a bed would come first. I knew where the closest shelter was, so I headed off in that direction, hoping I wasn't too late to get myself some kind of comfortable mattress for the night.

I arrived on 5th Ave, looking straight at the crowd already in line for a bed and a free meal. I moved slowly towards that line, hoping that I would be accepted and that I wasn't too late.

I shimmied in behind this enormous Mexican lady, right at the end of the line. I was now last in line, but very soon there would be many more behind me.

I tapped her on the shoulder.

"You think I will get a bed?" I asked

She ignored me, and then spat on the ground, a huge ball of phlegm, released with venom.

"Charming!" I said, "what the fuck is your problem?" I asked her, knowing I had to act tough to get the respect I so craved. This was part of the law of this jungle. Be vocal and remain vocal and perhaps, just maybe, someone would listen. She didn't want to listen though, and turned her back to face the front of the line again.

'Oh well' I thought, 'I tried."

Bodies were gathering behind me, one after another, moving in tandem with the flow of humanity that would eventually go no place and no place fast. Step, step, stutter, stutter. The guy behind me, a black guy, 5 ft 3 inches at the most and with a huge fat belly, just kept staring at me. I thought at one point he was going to shoot me with his superpower laser beam eyes, but of course, that never happened. It was extremely disconcerting and it took everything I had in the way of patience, not to kick him in the balls and tell him to stop staring.

5 PM, on the dot, the line began to move.

5.15 PM, I was already inside the building.

5.25 PM, I had a bed.

5.30 PM, I was being fed.

5.50 PM, I was finished and asked to return to the bunk house.

6PM, the fun began.

Some Say Nuts

Minus two, perhaps minus some common sense
Standing, waiting, anticipating
Fifty or more ahead of the game
Patiently expectant
Some might say nuts
Holding on to their dream
Keeping warm as entry beckoned

Precisely nine and not one minute more
Doors wide open in the face of happiness
Warmth now just around the corner
Heat of battle no longer an issue
Marching to the beat of success
Winding towards victory
Arriving, at last, in dreamland

One by one, smiles broader than their chest
Leaving, gloating, proud
New owners of this 'hard to get' trophy
Carried with pride, maybe some confusion
Wondering why and for what reason
Offering no answers
Plodding onwards to complete temporary fulfillment

Fun times, NOT!

Rape, yes rape, pillage, theft, abuse, smoking, drug use, alcohol abuse. It all kicked off. By 6.30 PM, I was so fucking scared, I almost shit my pants. Everywhere, and I mean everywhere, something bad was going down. Realizing that there are too many mental health issues to count when it comes to the homeless population in America, successive governments sharing in their responsibilities for canceling mental health programs around the country, leading to an expansion of the lunatic fringe on our, not so safe streets, the place I was about to go to sleep in, and yes, I was absolutely exhausted, exploded into what I can only describe as total mayhem.

As I watched out of my wide open eyes, I witnessed things that I could hardly believe. I'd read about these places before I'd decided to be homeless for that week, never doubting it would be a challenge for mild-mannered old me to cope. When I actually experienced what was going on, live and in person, believe me, it placed a new meaning on violence, corruption and unabated crime.

One guy, a white guy, came from one side of the room, smashing his way across several bunk beds, caring little for who was lying there or what they had beside them in the way of belongings, got to the other side of that room, walked up to a female, she was about 45 years old, punched her directly in the face, knocking her flat on her bunk, got on top of her, too out his penis and began masturbating on top of her. As he did this, some of the staff, armed with nothing but brawn and no brains, rushed to the woman's aid, trying hard to pull this idiot off of her and almost losing their own lives as some of the other men in the room took charge and joined in the fun, also trying to decapitate them. This was a hate, hate situation, compounded by intoxication and drug addiction that seemed to engulf all who cared to participate, other than the staff, of course. What a mess. The battle ensued for a minute or two, at which point, a man with a whistle entered the room.

A huge shrill of that whistle soon brought the carnage to an end. The mess was there for all to see. Belongings strewn all over the place, vomit and blood everywhere, and one or two, mostly mean unwelcoming faces, being escorted right out the door, no discussion, no way back in. The woman, yes THAT woman, the one with the man on top of her, was taken away to receive medical attention, and from the look on her face, she needed it, and needed it badly.

My decision at that moment in time was whether to stay or to flee. The previous evening on the grass at the park seemed lame in comparison to what I'd just witnessed and my mind, unable to switch off the gore from the scene that had just taken place, suggested to the rest of my body that it was time to flee. Having said that, this, technically, was research and in the end, I stayed.

I laid back on the bunk, fully clothed, my radar on full throttle, taking in each and every person who was surrounded me, mannerisms and mental state, then computing that against the awful scenes from a few minutes' prior and then, finally, deciding in my brain who I thought I could trust and who I knew I should avoid.

It was very early and the night was going to be long and interesting and honestly, I needed to sleep. The question was, would I?

By 7 PM, a kind of gentle hush had prevailed as everyone began to settle down for the night. There are strict rules in all of these shelters, but a lot of those rules are broken frequently, and without punishment. I soon discovered that no sex and no drug use meant nothing to some and as the evening drew to a close, the noise from people snoring, farting, burping, talking to themselves, was almost unbearable.

The lights go out, (at least that's what they say, lighting is always on in some form or other), at 9 PM, which suited me. I was ready to sleep, no one else was. I lay down, again, carefully scrutinizing anyone within spitting distance of where my bed was, and thinking only about survival. My 'stash', I hoped was still hidden and untouched, and I vowed to go and reclaim it at dawn. In the meantime, I was saddened by the depravity which now surrounded me. 400 souls, lost and lonely, and with no one in their lives to snuggle up to or to just touch. That's one thing about being homeless and alone, you lose the luxury of touch. Seen as a leppers in our society, there's an anxiousness when confronted by a 'normal' person, a reason to take a step back and to keep one's distance. Not only because you know you smell, which 100% of the homeless I met did, and with some distinction too, but because you know you want and need a hug, and you know even better, or have learned fairly quickly, that hug will never arrive. Some of these homeless souls go 20 to 30 years without the luxury of human touch. How sad must that be? Something you and I take for granted, but something they will receive only as a distant memory.

My eyes began to close, and although my trust surrounding my neighbors was never completely fulfilled, exhaustion overcame my weary body and I fell asleep.

Where Is It Going

Collected in bag fulls from every corner
As I sit, watching this madness continue
In a small seat on a large tube
Just one little part of a huge problem
Asking oneself continuously, where does it all go?

Bagged up and discarded, precariously
One on top of another
Some sense of sadness accompanying relief
My problems, minor in comparison
Really convinced of mismanagement

Landing safely and breathing fresh air
Looking left and right for anything to join me
Suddenly confronted by a notion
Sensing doom from the idea of complete revulsion
Saddened by the larger picture, the black and the white

No solution, no attempt, no answers
All hurried deep within rotting earth
Casually ignoring a direction of safety
Madness, from within souls who crave cleanliness
Compromising the future in favor of a simple present

No breakfast at 2 AM, no one to talk to and no way to get out. Simple but true. I was stuck, wide awake, listening to sounds that one can only dream of, and none of them very nice. There was one man in particular who just talked to himself all night. No matter how many times other people would tell him to 'shut up', he just carried on and on and on. He was mentally ill of course, but after listening to the same crap for hours on end, he was making everyone else ill too. So sad, so unfortunate, so utterly desperate. I got out of bed, walked around the room a little, only to find that I'd raised the annoyance level of those slightly asleep and those slightly awake. One thing I learned early on was that sleep, if it wasn't drug induced or forced on by over excretion with Jim Beam or the likes, didn't really ever come easy to anyone who was homeless. They all tended to have one eye open while sleeping, just in case. Violence was rife, and so was theft. Everyone was wary, including me. For hours I lay on my bunk, trying to imagine what it would be like to do this day in and day out. Sleep never returned and by 6 AM, I was up and out of there, hoping that at some point in my week I'd find someplace better than this. I left that shelter feeling dirtier and more exhausted than when I'd arrived. The question now was, what should I do and where should I go? My stash, yes, that fabulous collection I'd accumulated the previous day. It needed to be checked and without too much else to do at that time of the morning, I headed straight back to where I'd hidden it. I still had about $4 hidden in my shoe and breakfast at Micky Ds sounded like a plan and a real treat. I also needed to poop and brush my now, disgustingly dirty, teeth. Thankfully, after a 15-minute walk, I found my stash was still hidden and intact. I'd put a bottle of water inside one of the sweaters, which I removed and gulped down in less than a minute leaving just a little to brush my teeth with. While I drank, I stood contemplating my options. Should I leave my things here, or take them with? Would anyone care either way? I didn't really fancy carrying them around all day and as they'd been safe overnight, there was nothing to suggest they wouldn't remain safe throughout the day. I packed them up, ditched them and walked off in search of something to eat and perhaps a local 'early riser' who might just spare me a dollar or two. At that time of day, commuters were arriving by the boat load, literally! They came in on designated ferries from Tiburon, Sausalito and other places north of the city. Occupied by those who were smart enough not to commute by car, and the traffic nightmare the Golden Gate Bridge could often be, those ferries afforded me a fabulous opportunity to panhandle for cash and then hopefully find some nice food to buy with that cash, to keep me going all day. Having been up since around 2AM, I knew it was going to be very difficult to stay awake and alert all day and that a nap of some kind, whether it was under a tree, on a piece of grass or just propped up against a building, was going to be a necessity. I moved quickly and as unobtrusively as possible towards the soon to be crowded Ferry building, which, I hoped, would breathe life into my wanning cash situation.

The throngs of people I'd imagined arriving bright and early for work, was just in the process of ramping up from its early morning staggered but quiet beginning, to a full-on rush. That rush would take place over the 7 to 8 AM timeframe. I was arriving just in time, willing and very ready to put on my best face and place my hands out in front of all those potential dollars that could mean survival for me and a more relaxed approach to what would obviously become another tedious day.

Couldn't Care Less

A half empty sack of hope thrown across an aching back
Carried with attitude from one side to another
Aware that his turn was yet to come
Happy to break the rules in favor of chance
Remaining calm whilst those in a rush became agitated

Perhaps rendered deaf by a will to ignore
Horns and verbal abuse flung at the speed of his slow walk
Choosing to smile rather than frown
Hitting the other side of nowhere as slowly as possible
Watching how upset his aggressors could really get

With little to look forward to and nothing to look back upon
Careless abandonment of all common sense
Prevailing winds pushing him towards nothing in particular
Emptiness as vast as his life to date
Carrying only the burden of those who wait impatiently behind
his gentle footsteps

An eventual arrival signaling continuation for those who have plenty
Intimidating in their gestures as life goes on
Pushing hard towards meaningless destinations
Ignorant of the plight that bad luck can bring
Forgetting rapidly that human being they nearly destroyed

The art of begging isn't something that anyone should take for granted. Begging's origins go back thousands of years, if not tens of thousands, and should not necessarily be associated with just poor homeless people looking for handouts. I have seen people, many people, asking for cash when they look like they have on the best shoes and the nicest clothes and don't really need it. Often there are no rules for those looking to gain favor from other people's naivety or willingness to be Christian and kind. Begging can be seen daily, all over the world, and in all walks of life and it doesn't need to be for money, or food. I remember begging one of my clients to give me his business because my production plant at that time was on the verge of liquidation. Thankfully he complied and we survived, but only just.

There are also people in government, people who are married, people who have great jobs, people who are just feeling sad, who beg. Beg for forgiveness, for another chance, for many things we don't, as human beings, recognize as begging, in its literal sense. But begging is an art form, one that can be easily mastered and one that is often misunderstood, and certainly one that can bring great benefits to its aficionados.

In the ferry building there were two men that I noticed immediately as I walked inside the huge open front door. One was to the right and the other to the left. Both looked like any other homeless person on these streets, but there was something about the one on the right that struck me as being different or unusual. I also noticed that both were dressed similarly, almost like twins, and both had on very nice-looking Nike shoes, which were clean and very new looking. I was curious, very curious, and while people passed me by, lots of people, all with potential to give me money, I ignored the throngs and concentrated on these two guys who had not become more than just a fascination to me. I knew something wasn't right, but I couldn't put my finger on it. I watched them closely, and after about 25 minutes, I figured it out, at least I thought I'd figured it out.

The one on the left of the building had a sign held out right in front of him, again, the sign looked new, not disheveled like most signs you'd see held by anyone who was genuinely homeless or down on their luck. You know the kind? A piece of carboard out in front of them with a few words scrawled in felt tip pen. No, his sign was almost professional. It was pristine, with a sparkling white background and beautifully written words, all in line and all spelt correctly. There was nothing on this sign or the way this guy looked that spelled out homeless to me. The other guy, on the right was even more interesting. He was clean shaved and actually looked like he'd bathed, not just in the last few hours, but regularly over the past months. Not sure how I could tell, but I was pretty certain these guys were not homeless, and at that moment in time my intuition was guiding me to that conclusion.

I decided to explore further.

Slowly I approached the guy on the left, moving in towards him and his 'little corner' that he'd sort of marked off as his very own. 'This was going to be very interesting', I thought.

"Yo!" I nodded towards him.

"What?" he replied.

"You having any luck?" I could see from the tray laid out in front of his feet that he'd been very successful so far, and it wasn't even 8 AM!

"Hey, what the fuck do you want man?" he said.

"Oh, I am thinking of setting up right here, right next to you" I said, at which point his facial expression changed and his attitude became very aggressive.

"Get the fuck away from me man. I was here first. I don't need you crowding in my territory" he was definitely shouting now and the passing commuters were avoiding a possible confrontation that was definitely looming. You could tell from their eyes, which seemed to be pointing down to the floor of the ferry building, that they wanted to get outside and away from the two of us, and with some urgency. The guy from the right of the building noticed what was going on and he started to walk towards us. At this point, I feared the worse. These two were cohorts for sure. I knew it, I'd felt it and now I was about to experience it, first hand.

Both guys were showing signs of aggression but with the ferry building quite busy, for some reason I felt quite safe. I wasn't sure what they were thinking but as Righty approached, the verbal onslaught he let go, was something to be laughed at, only because it was so perfectly eloquent! There was no slurring of words, not too much in the way of profanity and a slight, if not daring, attempt to be civil. Lefty, on the other hand, well, he went for it. Full on, profanity laden diatribe, without any care or concern for anyone who might want to listen, including kids, who were also walking through that building at the time.

As Righty marched over, and as Lefty was in full swing with his expletive tirade, I put both arms up in the air, as if I was surrendering to a man with a gun pointed at my head. I decided at that point to approach Righty, who had moved and was almost right bang in front of me.

"You guys aren't homeless! Are you??"

"Who the fuck are you to ask?" said Lefty, who was now starting to calm down a little.

"I just know" I said, "listen guys, I am not here to steal anything from you, nor am I here to question what you're doing. I am NOT homeless, I am up here because I want to be, not because I need to be. All I want to know, and I'll explain if you both calm down, is how long you've been doing this, what kind of life you guys have, and why you do it?"

Lefty and Righty looked at one another. They were absolutely and utterly confused.

Righty, "Fuck you and fuck whoever sent you! You a cop?"

Me, "No, FUCK YOU and fuck you for taking from those who really need it. And NO, I am a writer"

Lefty, "Fuck us?? You write what?"

Me, "A book about homelessness, but I couldn't write it without trying it. Being homeless, that is. This is my 3rd day. I have worked with homeless people for over 25 years and I knew when I walked in here an hour ago that you guys weren't homeless. Now, I'm not here to judge or to tell you to get out, or indeed to suggest anything else to you guys. I just want to chat to see if there's anything you can tell me that would look good in my book and also help me get some food and advise me the best places to go to stay at night"

Calm prevailed, but skepticism was written right across both of their faces. They were so confused.

Righty, "Listen man, it's rush hour. Come back in 45 minutes, we can talk"

Lefty, "Yeah, fuck off, get yourself a coffee someplace and come back. We busy. Got it?" and with that statement, he made that international sign of a blade cutting his own throat, the first sign of real aggression, aimed towards me of course.

Me, "OK I will be back at 8.45. Don't go anywhere, because now I know where to find you both, and one thing I can't stand, is someone who says one thing and does another. So, you guys hang out until I get back! Please????"

Lefty, "Where you from man?"

I laughed at him and said, "take a guess, and it's not Oakland!"

Eden's Gate

Keeper of Eden's gate
Where are you now?
Leaving unlocked, the key to all life
Set forth to multiply
Unwilling to respect
On the run as a herd
Unwilling to compromise
Fearing no one, other than those who dissent
Tied up in times of change
Losing rapidly their will to believe

Rounding up those chosen few
Placed in a meaningless position
Pleading endlessly for change
Willing to play leper
Unfazed by challenge
Reminders of past fulfillment
Now plagued by dogma
Set in stone, though carved like ice
New shepherds in a new world
Unable to round up vanishing tribes

Breakfast! I was starving, and I needed to eat.

"Any chance I can borrow a few bucks' mate?"

I was standing right next to a dapper looking 20 something year old, someone who I'd inadvertently bumped into as I left the ferry terminal. It was a complete accident, but the guy was so shocked and so determined to get out of my way that he took a note out of his trouser pocket and thrust it into my hand without checking to see what it was. $20! I was rich and raring to go. I could eat anywhere, even a nice diner, but again, who the heck would let me in dressed this way, and smelling like a sewer? I was also on a time limit, having made it clear to Righty and Lefty that I'd return to finish our conversation. I opted for fast food, yet again and I knew that at this rate, my bowels would explode from all the crap I was eating.

I spent $5, kept the rest, making a total of around $19 in my shoe, and headed back to confront the gruesome twosome.

They were still inside the ferry building, and by the looks of things, doing quite well. The morning rush was now tailing off and their task was seemingly over for yet another day. As I walked in, turning left towards Righty, I could tell they were both very annoyed I'd returned, but I'd told myself that I needed to try to find out what the heck these guys were actually doing. It was fascinating to me that two men, certainly intelligent and obviously not homeless, chose to do this 'panhandling lark' each and every day. 'It must be lucrative' I thought to myself, and it must keep them both financially stable for them to stand there day after day? I asked Righty, if he and Lefty would like to go for a quick walk, or perhaps sit on a bench and chat?

Both were reluctant to do so, but after some Scottish charm, and a few jokes, they agreed.

It turned out to be an extremely enlightening conversation, on a park bench, one which I promised I would never reveal, hence the delay in publishing this book some 14 years after meeting them, and of course, changing their identities. I'm sure, if they're still alive and still frequenting the same building daily, anyone reading this now will have no issue identifying them should they want to try, but I believe enough time has passed for both to have moved on, and this is why.

Lefty, "So, you're writing a book?"

Me, 'Yes, but no idea if it'll ever get published"

Lefty," How'd you know we were faking it?"

Me, "I worked with homeless people for many years. I had a hunch you guys weren't without a roof over your heads. So, tell me, what's the real story?"

Righty, "Why should we tell you or trust you?"

Me, "You shouldn't, but if you don't it's not going to be difficult for me to write about you now. I could sell the story to one of the local papers, and expose you?" I lied. I would never have done that, but I wanted their story and I had to see how far I could push them before they either got up and walked away, or just hit me.

The floodgates opened, and as they both told me their stories, I could see that there was some relief on their faces as their concealed truth came tumbling out. It took over an hour for them to narrate their plight, if one can call it that, as adults, which had led to several failed attempts in business and insecurity at their workplace because of color and race. In the end, Lefty admitted he'd watched panhandlers beg for money for years and the two of them had cracked this crazy scheme that would lead them to join the ranks of San Francisco's homeless population each day, hands out, begging for cash. Both of them split their earnings and according to Righty, they took in over $100,000 a year, tax free! They both lived in homes outside the city, both had cars, both had families and both were happy to pay zero tax on any of their earnings while also enjoying and collecting unemployment benefits each week.

What a scam, I thought, what a bloody liberty. But, you know, at the end of the day, if they can pull it off, well, good luck to them. At least they're trying. I asked them straight up, "are you worried about being caught?"

Both just laughed, and replied in unison, "Who is ever going to catch us?"

Rules Of Life

Nothing is the same
All men are not equal
Some are fitter and stronger
Others larger and plumper

Some of us get sick
Others get sicker
Two degrees colder and you are gone
Two degrees warmer completes the demise

Kids suffer from incurable diseases
Tyrants can live a healthy life
The innocents that suffer
No crimes in their past

Some steal and they do not deserve
Others deserve and do not take
Even distribution impossible
Greed amongst us too strong

Doing good for many
No guarantees of goodness in return
Decisions made for us by chance
Fairness not a priority

There are no rules in life
No checklist of wrongs and rights
Flying by the seat of our pants
Guided by destiny

One thing's for sure, other than Lefty and Righty, there were many other people doing the same thing. I met a few, but never delved as deeply into their business as I did with L and R. One other thing I did learn, although not that particular day, I think it was day 6 when I uncovered this one.

Traffic light windshield washers.

They come out of nowhere when cars are stationary at a red light and ask the driver if they want their windshield washed. You know who they are, we've all been victims. You say no, and they just continue to wash your window, most with a threatening look of 'you better tip me or I'll dent your car.'

It's all a scam. These guys are run by pimps. They are rotated around their cities every two hours and appear at different traffic lights in the same cities, all at varying times, splitting their cash with the guy who pimps them. They do this every day, and we, the drivers, are funding them. They are not homeless. They are exploited, mostly by unscrupulous thugs taking advantage of immigrants.

Anyway, with day 3 off to a flyer and with cash in hand, I had a choice. I was thinking that the Marina district might be a good bet to meet more of my touristy friends and make some money or, maybe just hang around Fisherman's Wharf one more day, just to see what happens. I eventually decided to hang around the wharf and save day 4 for the Marina.

Picking a spot is always crucial when it comes to begging, picking the right spot, and not getting in anyone's way or invading someone else's territory. It's a process of elimination for sure, but something I learned to do very quickly. You have to stake out the area you choose, being careful to ensure that there are no infringements on territory that belongs to regular panhandlers and their cohorts. It's difficult at first to determine who is a regular and who deserves to be where they're actually sitting or standing, and yes, there is a pecking order, an enforced line up, but after a few quick lessons from Oleg on day 1, I was becoming a total pro. Navigating this minefield eventually became second nature to me. In fact, even today, all these years later, I am confident I could walk on to any street, knowing who was regular and who wasn't.

Apart from shoes, or lack thereof, the first signs one should look for when trying to determine who is genuinely homeless and who isn't, are skin abrasions and deterioration, and also a person's teeth. Sun damage, wind damage, lack of nutrition, all lead to yellow, pitted, ageing skin. Teeth, from lack of dental care, are also a dead giveaway, but honestly, shoes are always my first go to. See a guy standing at a traffic light? Check out his shoes. If they're good, move along and do not give. See someone on the streets begging, same applies. Yes, it's a cruel evaluation to have to make and sometimes I suppose, there are those who have managed to beg borrow or steal new shoes, but this isn't an everyday occurrence, so stick with my theory before donating, and you'll rarely, if ever go wrong.

The wharf that morning was busy, and eventually I picked my spot and waited. I had all day after all. What else was I going to do? Exactly! Nothing!

Panhandling is like everything else in life, patience, of which I have little. However, as I sat perusing the crowds and as tourists began appearing, fresh from a good night's sleep on their comfortable hotel beds, I was taken aback by how brazen some of the seasoned beggars could be. No patience and all and right in for the kill. Success rate? Less than 3 % was my calculation. I kept a mental note of all the panhandlers in my sight, watching closely as they sat, walked and deliberately molested the crowds. Donations were obviously at a premium and fights were looming amongst those who felt that they, and they only, should be the worthy recipients of a very limited and always dwindling, cash pool.

Two elderly gents, both smelling like sewers, (and I knew this because both had walked past me twice), began the proceedings.

Their beef seemed to be all over a dollar bill, a single dollar bill, which to them would seem like a million dollars, but in this case, this dollar, the one that was now stuck between both guys sets of hands, was being pulled left and right and up and down, as the survival of the fittest took its toll. I got fed up listening to the expletives coming from each of their potty mouths and in the interest of détente, I decided to intervene. Big mistake!

"For fucks sake you two, it's $1, split it" is what I said as I marched up and stood next to them.

The look of disbelief on both was evident, each one pondering what the heck was going on and who this foreigner, (who was obviously speaking in a different language), thought he was and why was he interrupting their battle?

I tried again.

"Gentlemen, what the fuck are you fighting over $1 for?"

Yellow face, the taller of the two, although both were shorter than me, gave me a look and said, "Fuck you, and fuck him too", as he pointed to black face. The color of their faces didn't depict their race by the way, this was genuinely their color, probably from drugs and lack of bathing. Both men were indeed white.

Then the brawl began, real fisticuffs. Yellow attacked black, black stepped back and aimed a drunken left hook at yellow, both men seemed inebriated, and probably were. Black then tried to kick yellow, and yellow, having sidestepped the kick, fell immediately down, as if a sniper had shot him. He then began to roll around on the ground screaming obscenities at no one in particular. None of this made any sense. Black tried to jump on top of yellow, but he couldn't make that happen. His feet seemed glued to the ground. His knees were bending, his face and body looked like they were trying to jump, but he remained stuck to the sidewalk. It was hilarious to everyone watching, including me. I decided to put a swift end to this farce by taking another $1 from the stash in my shoe and presenting it to both of them. "Here!" I said, "now there are two $1 bills. Take one each and piss off back to where you came from, but stop this nonsense now."

The fight halted, but black, still on the same spot and still trying to jump on yellow, looked at the $1, grabbed it from me and walked off, his legs now, miraculously, working. Yellow, lying on the sidewalk, had the other $1, and now that black had left the scene, he jumped up, shouting in the direction of a retreating black, "victory, victory, fuck off you homo bastard". It was over, and it was time to go back to my seat on the monument that I'd commandeered. By then, the large crowd, which had gathered to watch the 'big' fight, began dispersing. A woman in her late 50's came towards me with an outstretched arm and a greenback of some denomination in her hand.

"This is for you" she said, and thrust it into my left palm. She didn't stop to chat, she just walked away. I looked down and saw the $5 bill she'd just given me was brand new and very crisp. What a profit! I'd stopped a fight by giving up a dollar, and gained by receiving $5. The day could only go downhill after that!

Dirt Following Dirtier

Blue, well it used to be, now brown
A yellow mess, sort of black
Green teeth, at least from a distance
Torn leather, on black, or maybe brown shoes
Matted grey and greasy orange hair
Two steps in front, showing male dominance
This was dirt following dirtier

Carrying the burden of a lover's tiff
Shouting insults, with head popped backwards
Screaming silently into a breeze
Laughed at, cautioned and then cajoled
Unwilling to concede
Walking faster then slower and then faster once again
Unable to break their bond, this filthy marriage

An audience of transients, amused
One or two in a state of shock
Many just ignoring this sideshow of intolerance
Some, perhaps having been willing participants of their own
Willing them on, to the bitter end
Sensing more entertainment, from exceedingly bad breath
Putrid stench of victory, impossible to smell

Sitting down, jeans and shorts, ripped and ragged
Peace, moments away in a kiss
Hand in hand to the tune of silent applause
Make up time, over a half-eaten sandwich
Sharing bites, and apologies
Him, happy, her, hungry
Both sad, homeless and in need of a clean up

Time passes so slowly when you have nothing to do but sit and watch life go by. Some of the people I'd met though were always busy. Collecting this and that from trash cans, walking up and down the same streets dozens of times a day, talking to themselves continuously from dawn to dusk and even into the night. Some of those very same people were in wheelchairs, some had limbs missing, some were ex-army, navy or air force, and most had medical or psychological issues that were obviously beyond repair, which, honestly, was the saddest thing I ever witnessed. If only someone else other than all those good Samaritans, cared. And then there are government do-gooders, doing NO good at all. If only there was a way to house some of our homeless, giving them back their dignity, their self-respect, and most importantly, a purpose in their lives. Having worked in shelters and having talked to hundreds of homeless victims, from vets in wheelchairs, to ladies and gentlemen who lost their partners, husbands, wives, and couldn't cope with huge medical bills they inherited, to kids, who's only fault in being homeless was the fact that their parents had lost all hope, to respectable and very clever men and women, suffering from a breakdown or from some other medical or mental problem, the same story prevailed. Give them hope, self-respect, a purpose in life and perhaps, just perhaps, we can reduce the incredible numbers that now live on our streets. It was while I was sitting at the wharf that afternoon that I came up with a plan, the Zoltie plan, a plan I believe could put a huge dent in the ever-expanding homeless population in America, reducing its numbers by more than half. I know there are and always will be those who want to be homeless. Those who enjoy it or who do it to remain off-grid in a political system they do not agree with, and I am not naïve enough to believe that my plan could actually work, but it's a plan that's so different from anything else that's ever been attempted, and everything else to date has failed, therefore my plan, the Zoltie plan, needs to be addressed and discussed and perhaps implemented, on the off-chance I may have concocted something that might just actually work. That plan? Well, more about the plan towards the end of this book.

My day 3, on Pier 39 became more than interesting after I watched one lady, a small fat lady, pushing a shopping cart with all of her worldly belongings off the end of the pier and into the water, breaking the fence that was placed there just to prevent stupidity such as this. She didn't care, and as she shouted one profanity after another at the cart, while she smashed it several times against this fence, eventually for the fence to give way and the cart to drop 30 feet into the bay, I honestly believed she was going to follow it. The commotion she caused, as two cops arrived and dragged her away, possibly to the closest asylum, was horrendous. When they eventually got her into the back of the cop car, (one cop had arrived on a bike), she'd lost most of her clothing and was as naked as the day she'd been born, only wrinklie! What a piece of work this woman turned out to be and although I felt sorry for the cops, the tourist contingent who were around the pier and ready and willing to be entertained by more than just those street magicians and musicians who are ever-present on Pier 39, well they just loved the soap opera that unraveled in front of them. Many of them taking pictures, some clapping, some laughing, even though there was nothing very funny about what was going down. Tourists are weird like that. A scene unfolds, just as it does on TV in their home country, and they all think it's marvelous entertainment from America, and just like CSI Miami or the likes. They believe that this is the reality of every-day USA. It's what America offers, as seen on all of their own countries news programs and now, here it was, live and in person and ready to be enjoyed in the flesh. Thank God it wasn't that woman's flesh though! She was horrible, smelly and disgustingly vile both from her looks and the crap pouring out of her mouth. I really think the police are undervalued and underpaid.

They carted her off and things calmed down. I was hungry again, and needed food, but not fast food this time. Too much of that and I knew I'd be ill for weeks. More cash guaranteed better food, and while the police were wrapping up their duties with that lady and her cart, I approached a couple who were watching the event unfurl, believing, rightly or wrongly that they were from Israel. I thought I'd heard a smidgeon of Hebrew and I decided to try my luck with them to see if I could get them to cough up some money. I speak a little of that language and when I approached them, I knew my purpose began with my element to surprise, something I'd learnt, brought in fast money.

"Ma'shlomcha?" (how are you?) I asked in Hebrew as I drew closer to 2 very surprised and smiling Israeli's.

Garbage Of Life

The garbage of life lays strewn across deserted streets
Putrid smells of decaying waste
Hanging in the air from block to block
Unavoidable odors of disgusting proportion
Human and man-made, discarded throughout the night

A new day awakening to the same trash
Broken bags, contents half eaten by rodents
Scampering to safety as first light breaks through gray clouds
Filled and satisfied from their night long pillaging
Retreating quickly to the sewers where they thrive

From nowhere they arrive en-mass
Trucks, with arms that grasp, driven by men in brown
Entering this arena of filth, ready to do battle
Cleansing the sidewalks in swift methodical movements
Relieving the city of its burden

Before long an unwanted task is performed
Returning home to dispose of their bounty
Bringing a breath of fresh air to those who rise late
Unaware of the chaos preceding them
Leaving a sense of security, as perfection is returned.

We conversed in broken Hebrew for a few minutes, my secondary language skills being extremely limited, and then we switched to English, of which they were fluent. After going back and forth with the usual questions, who do you know, why are you here, there's only 6000 Jews in Scotland, etc, they gave me $100 and wished me all the best as they walked away. I'd offered them tourist advice, restaurant recommendations and suggestions for Vegas, their next stop, none of which they wanted to take. They just wanted to give a poor Jewish guy some Tzedakah, (charity).

I was so tempted to tell them why I was really there, but I couldn't force myself to break cover. I think they thought I was nuts and felt sorry for me, but whatever they thought and no matter how bad they felt, if you guys are reading this now, I am very grateful for what you did for me that day. Rhone and Ari were their names. It's a long time ago but hopefully somewhere somehow, this chapter will find them in good health and thriving. My $100 was a complete windfall, but also a curse. What does a homeless person do with a $100 note? It's hard enough to walk into a store with a $5 bill and buy something, but with $100? The looks I would get would probably range from 'thief' to 'forger' and to buy something for $1 and get $99 in change? Where would I hide all that cash? My intentions were to give away some of the money to homeless people I thought really needed it. It's easy to spot the one's that are in dire straits, and I'd had experience of this over the years.

In the early 2000's the noughties, as they are known in the UK, I used to drive up to San Francisco on Christmas week. I did this for about 5 years. I brought with me, $2000 in small bills and $1000 in large bills, and I walked the city for a day, handing out cash to those in need. I had certain criteria which determined who I would give to and who was most deserving of my generosity. I never told friends or family I was doing this, trying hard always, to preserve my anonymity. Sometimes you just need to give and give anonymously. During this period of giving, I learned rapidly who needed what and I learned that not all homeless people are equal. If I found a family with children, normally living in cars, I would hand out more than I would to a 'so called' bum at a street corner who was quite often obnoxious or perhaps high. It was tough not to give to everyone, because at some point in time, everyone is deserving, but decisions need to be made when funds are limited and, just like in battle, there are always casualties. If I'd had millions to give, I would have done so, and done so more liberally, but, at that point in my life, my 'fuck-you' money (fuck-you money is money you can afford to give away without even thinking about losing it), was limited. Learning the city, at that point in my life, was also a curious, although rewarding experience which stood me in good stead for this particular week when I, myself, was homeless. I knew what places to avoid, what to do for shelter, where the gangs roamed, and also where all those with kids who were homeless parked their cars at night. When my day handing out cash was over, each year I would feel worse than the previous year. The first year I felt that I'd done something worthwhile and rewarding. By the end of the 5th year of doing this, I was distraught and devastated by a situation that had become a pandemic and a pandemic I had no chance of making even the smallest of dents in. The homeless population at that time was large, now, it's huge and getting worse by the day, and even though I might change someone's life for a few hours, they have years, if not a lifetime of misery in front of them, misery that will never change or recede. It's just heartbreaking, or at least it was. So, I stopped going up at Christmas time, hoping I could find a better, more effective and fair way to dilute or ease the pain for the tens of thousands of men women and children I couldn't help. That solution came in the form of this book. I figured that if I could sell one book for every homeless person in America, some 2.5 million, all the proceeds could go directly to them, to their pockets, and not to charities, all of whom are trying hard to cope with their lack of funding, and fight daily to decide who should benefit and who shouldn't. I wanted to be the owner of my destiny, and therefore the destiny of so many who have no hope and no way out. This by the way, isn't my plan to cure homelessness for good. No, this is just a stepping stone on my road to being able to make that attempt. Those days of walking up and down-Market St, the Tenderloin, and such, were filled with amazing stories that could fill another book, but one story in particular from that time, a story that still brings a tear to my eye, was when I met a Hispanic couple parked up in a free parking spot near the Marina. The story begins with me approaching the vehicle, seeing two kids in the back seat and their parents, speaking in English with a few words of Mexican Spanish thrown into each sentence.

"Hugo, please get out and use the inodoro (toilet), it's getting late and almost time to banos (bathe)" said the father. I caught this Spanglish discussion very briefly as I passed their vehicle, noticing the two small kids in the back seat were preparing their blankets as if they were about to go to bed. I found this very strange indeed because, although I'd heard of kids and adults being homeless and sleeping in cars, I'd never actually witnessed it first-hand. This would be my first time, and certainly not my last. I had been in the city since early morning handing out cash, and I was ready to go home. I had $200 left to donate and was searching high and low for the perfect recipients, when this situation, a situation that was dreadful to witness, came into view and then up close and in person. I was stunned at how this family were living and felt the urge to move on without talking to them, fearing that if I did stop and chat, I might regret it. This feeling was purely from a selfish standpoint as I didn't want to interrupt what was clearly an evening routine for all of them. It was around 7 PM and it was cold, not freezing, but cold.

I stopped, taking my time to get closer to their truck, just to double check that my instincts had been correct and that indeed they were living in this vehicle.

"Hi" I said, the smile on my face depicting friend, not foe.

"Hola" came the restrained reply.

My next half hour was taken up chatting to the whole family. It turned out that they'd lost their home in San Raphael, north of San Francisco, due to a 'misunderstanding' with their landlord. The gist of that story, one I felt was genuine and sincere, was that the landlord felt the family were being disruptive by having their kids practice violin and trumpet during the early evening hours each day, when all his other renters demanded peace. He'd found a way to evict them, hoping because these people were probably illegal immigrants, (something I didn't dare delve into when conversing with them that day), there would be no negative feedback from any local government departments or advocates for the homeless and that the family would just vanish, never to be seen again. They'd been living on the streets for a month now, with the father, Jose, trying to find daily work to bring in cash for food and gas for the truck, and the mother, trying hard to homeschool her kids, either inside the car or on any patch of greenery she could find that day, depending on the weather. It was a mess, and a mess that was all too common around the state of California and probably the rest of country too.

"Listen" I said, "I have $200 here that I would like to give to you" The mother's eyes opened wide and she began to cry, "And", I continued, "I would like to try to help find you a place to live where you can all be safe."

Jose shook my hand and then he began to cry. Both kids were in the back seat of the truck, and when they saw their parents crying, they too started to cry. The vehicle they drove, a large truck, I believe was a Dodge, and their whole life was packed up inside the tail bed, including all the valuables they had and bedding and other small kitchen utensils. It was heartbreaking to see. The mother, and I forget her name now, was adamant that something good would happen to them, and I told her I would try very hard to make that good happen quickly. After giving them the $200, taking Jose's cell phone number, and promising them I would do my best to get back in touch quickly, I left for the evening and drove home to San Jose. I could not sleep for days and after several failed attempts at trying to contact social services in San Francisco, I eventually found someone in San Jose who thought they could pull a few strings. I am not sure how or when it happened, but about three months later, I called Jose.

"Jose, it's Alan, remember me?"

He did, and I could hear some excitement in his voice.

"Senior" he shouted, "muchas gracias, thank you, thank you, thank you. Because of you, I got a job and found a place to live"

"Because of me?" I questioned.

'Si, Alan, your friend called me and helped me"

"My friend?" I was lost here, either that or I had friends I didn't know about.

"Si, si, she call me, she meet me and she fixed everything. I now get job in construction, my wife make a new home in San Jose and my children go to school every day."

Well, I never really got the full story, but someone I'd called had called someone else and made something happen that was greater than any miracle I'd ever witnessed. Getting that family off the streets was an accomplishment, disproportionate to anything I had done. I'd only set the wheels in motion, thinking nothing would ever come of it. How wrong was I? Their lives had changed and changed for the better, I hoped, but there were tens of thousands just like that family, people you and I will never get to meet, but people who are suffering daily just to beat a system that is stacked against them. No job without an address. No address without a job! pathetic, but true. Welcome to western civilization, where very little is civil!

Living in Hope

An artificial sweat swept over a raised eye brow
Would he, or won't he?
If only telepathy worked
He prayed in silence
Egging on an act of self-defiance
Living in hope that this would be his day

He could smell their wealth
Feel the luxury that went with normality
Breathing in endless odors that had passed him by
Pondering, quite often, what it would be like
Brushing off their success as superficial
An excuse, perhaps, to live a lifestyle no one really required

"Go on" he mumbled under stale breath
Looking glum and sullen, never having to act
Smiling only as a brief thank you
A rarity amongst crowds that seldom gave
His saviors, lined up in droves, passing like ghosts
Determined to make his life more miserable by their lack of respect

Then it dropped, dropped like a bomb, but without noise
Commotion felt only inside a grateful heart
Unable to speak as his life improved ten-fold
Grabbing quickly this moment of deliverance
Pocketing what would become a weekly salary
Wiping away sweat that had now turned into tears of silent gratitude

Evening approached on day 3 and I still had my $100 bill, intact and unbroken. I'd spent the whole afternoon just walking around in a daze, trying hard to count as many homeless people as I could see. I'd reached 2400 when I gave up. Who knows if I counted anyone twice, but my thought process told me as long as I walked in a straight line, never returning to where I'd been, chances were good I had no doubles? I was hungry again, determined to give some of the $100 to other less fortunate homeless people, and pondering where I should sleep that night. Golden Gate Park was too far for me to walk, and as yet, I hadn't tried sleeping on the streets in a doorway, on a bench, or in a derelict building. It was time to make a choice. I stopped at small café near the marina, and walked in, knowing I'd probably get ejected fairly quickly.

"How's it going?" I said to the guy at the door who was standing waiting for customers to enter so he could seat them. It was still early and the dinner crowd hadn't begun to accumulate.

"Listen Boss" I continued, "I know I look homeless, but I'm not. I am up here from San Jose researching a book I'm going to write. I have money" and with that statement, I took out the $100 bill, "and have no problem paying. I know I stink, but that's what 3 days on the streets do to a man, so if it's OK with you, can I order something and eat it outside?"

The man wasn't only sympathetic but also very curious and we struck up an immediate conversation and rapport, after which, with me telling him my plans and my story so far, he fed me free of charge, gave me change for my $100 and even offered me a bed for the night in his home, which was about 15 minutes' walk from the café. What a gentleman!

I ate heartily, but turned down his offer of a bed, telling him that I needed to do it my way and remain homeless for as long as I'd promised myself. At the end of my meal, he shook my hand, offered me food whenever I needed for the rest of my stay in the city and also told me to let him know if he could give me more cash to hand out to those who needed it. What if it was that easy for anyone who was homeless? Pick a café, walk in, eat free, get cash handouts? It would put all those generous enough to participate, out of business in 5 minutes. Good souls are always hard to find, and when we do find them, they are few and far between and often underappreciated. That evening I was fortunate enough to have a full belly, the offer of a bed, which I of course turned down, and the inspiration that if more people like that existed, then perhaps, just perhaps, there was a small chance we might make the slightest of dents into a pandemic called depravity!

With the now 'broken' $100 in my pocket, I was off to find some deserving recipients before it got dark. I headed back towards my 'stash' of goodies that was still hidden, hopefully, and then to find a place to sleep for the night. The sun was once again setting and it was time to act before it got too dark to go anywhere. I didn't fancy staying around the wharf and as I mentioned, Golden Gate Park was just too far away for me to walk. I knew the city pretty well, and I also knew there was now no chance of persuading any shelter to take me in. It was just too late in the day for that. The good news was, I was fed and rested and if necessary, I'd just stay up all night, although having hardly slept a wink since I'd arrived two days earlier, the chances were slim I'd make it through another grueling day without some kind of rest. As I walked back to my hiding place, the city was filling up with tourists and locals, all looking for someplace to eat dinner, or on their way to watch one of the many shows that were playing in the local theatres or cinemas. Life was just normal for all of them, but for some, and I exclude myself from this category, life was just pure Hell, spending yet another night on streets they didn't want to be anywhere close to. These poor people, wrapped up in their own isolation. Self-inflicted or not, it was hard, very hard indeed, not to be sympathetic.

Methadone Madness

Standing up asleep and incoherent
Drifting backwards into methadone madness
Legs buckling towards an upside-down sky
Hitting the ground as the sun circles the moon
An unknown state of mindless fantasy
Arriving in moments and lasting into eternity

Formula, taken like a baby in need
Concocted over years in this recipe book of death
Numbing nodules, killing cells
Desecrating everything that makes any sense
Leaving torn and twisted remnants scratching for a cure
Disintegrating underneath watchful eyes

Weaned off nothing but common sense
Habitual users increasing an uncontrollable habit
Zombies, en-mass, providing proof of the living dead
Uncontrollable in an attempt to regain human status
Castigated, though impossible to ignore
Frightening the life out of those who have passed their way

Everything I'd left in my hiding spot was still there, neatly arranged and untouched. That made me very happy, although quite why anyone would even consider taking any of that stuff, was beyond me. Times were desperate, so you just never knew. Desperation always brought out the worst in human nature, as I'd already witnessed and these streets just reeked of desperate people. I took my stuff and headed out towards who knows where, hoping that life would just point me in the right direction. There were now some familiar faces on these streets. People I'd seen during the day, some at night but mainly homeless people who were walking back and forth to nowhere in particular. After all, where could they go to and never return? Nowhere. They were all stuck in their own bubble, a Groundhog Day that would last into eternity for most. I even passed Pinky and watched her beat the crap out of an older Asian homeless man. For what reason? I'd never find out, but the man was having the living daylights beaten out of him as he made no attempt to retaliate or even defend himself. I think he was drunk or worse, drunk and high, but he took the beating and then, as he lay there in a pool of his own blood, Pinky was being pulled away by some of her cohorts, just in time to receive another swig from yet another bottle. She was drunk for sure, drunk to the point of being uncontrollably violent. No one cared, not the police, not the tourists, not the locals, all having witnessed scenes like this and worse, all day, every day, 365 days a year. It just never ended, a vicious cycle of moronic uncontrolled violence, stemming from desperation, depravity, hunger, mental illness and so much more. How on earth could this ever be stopped. Even today, in 2022, there are over 50,000 homeless men, women and children, just in Los Angeles. And it's getting worse. These figures are increasing at a staggering rate, and although many have tried and indeed are still trying to tame this pandemic, nothing they do is helping. Some might say there are programs in place which are reducing numbers on these streets. Some might tell you that your dollars are making a difference. Some might even suggest that the issue of homelessness is something we shouldn't care about and that these people really want to be there. It's all nonsense. This is an issue that is not going away and is only going to get worse. As the 'haves' and 'have-nots' are segregated by such an enormous gap, the issue of homelessness is going to multiply tenfold in the coming 30 years. Possibly ending up as the worst humanitarian crises ever to hit the United States, even worse than illegal immigration, which is something that is also out of control. Stepping up now to try to resolve homelessness should be a priority in every state of the union. It's unfortunately not a priority with our federal government, who insist on spending billions on causes that make no sense and sending money to places that are not as deserving. Charity begins at home and it should be prioritized to stay at home until this pandemic is reversed.

Pinky was now in my rear-view mirror, so to speak, as I plodded on towards Ghirardelli square, where I thought I would try and find a place to sleep, down towards the rocks and steps that overlooked the island of Alcatraz. There's a kind of beach area there, but my hope was, that on the grass bank next to where the Lombard St cable car terminus lay, I would find a spot either next to or close by other homeless people who weren't looking to fight, get high, get drunk and just wanted to sleep. Tomorrow was going to be day 4, which left me three days total before I would return to San Jose and the comfort of my own home. These 3 days seemed like an eternity to me at that point, and sleep, something I needed now, and needed badly, would hopefully make those next few days more tolerable and less exhausting if I could at least get 4- or 5-hours rest.

The sweet smell of baking waffles filled the air as I approached the Ghirardelli chocolate shop, and as per usual, there was a line formed outside the door, everyone salivating in anticipation of the delightful treats they were about to devour. It seemed funny looking at this line and thinking I could join them if I wanted to, but my plans were to bed down and sleep. I headed for the grassy bank. There were of course already several other homeless men and women looking to do the very same thing and when I chose my patch of grass, my territory, I received the evil eye by one or two of them, obviously regular attendees at this very spot and having never seen me before, so very skeptical.

With my carboard laid flat, my blanket spread and my torn sweater as a pillow, I lay down and closed my eyes. It wasn't quite dark, and this was a very well-lit area, but that didn't matter. I was shattered, scared and also remorseful. It had been a real slog for me up until that moment, and something inside me just gave out. Something from within. Something that reminded me how fortunate I was and how unfortunate all of those sleeping next to me were. If I'd found just 3 days as a terrible hardship, how did these people cope with years sleeping rough? I just didn't get it. It seemed an impossible task, but one they all had to endure and one that most of them would never get out of. Poor bastards were stuck, stuck in a never-ending circle of shame and poverty.

I must have dozed off, because the next thing I knew I was being kicked in the feet. I awoke with a start, looking up to find a San Francisco cop, staring down at me. I was startled and a little scared.

"Move out man, you can't sleep here" he said.

"What time is it?" I asked.

"Midnight"

"Geez, I've been asleep for a couple of hours" I told him.

"Where are you from?" he asked

"Scotland, but that was a very long time ago" I replied

"What got you into this mess?" he said, as he pointed to all the sheets and cardboard around me.

"Oh," I said, "don't be fooled by all of this. I am researching a book and wanted to experience homelessness first hand, so I gave up my normal life for a week to see what it's like living out here on the streets"

"Are you mad?" he asked, as he laughed. By now, some of the other homeless bodies close by, were beginning to stir from their own slumber.

"Are you kicking all of them off this grass too?" I asked.

"Yep" he replied.

"I'd love to chat with you if you have the time. I would like your perspective on what's going on here and how you think we can resolve it." "I'll tell you what I'll do" he continued, "you see my car, it's parked up there" and he pointed towards a San Francisco police car, parked at the curb, just above where I was sleeping.

"Yep."

"Go up there, let yourself into the back seat and wait there for me. I'll be there in about 30 minutes."

And so, I did. I was very comfortable, at least I'd fallen asleep, on my little patch of grass, but obviously the city didn't want me there. I packed up and left, following his direction to sit in the back of the cop car. About 20 minutes passed and he returned.

"So" he said, as he made himself comfortable in the front seat, "tell me about your journey so far."

I told him what I'd been doing and where I planned to go tomorrow, or was it today? I then told him about my book, my passion to clear the streets of homeless people and the efforts I believe it would take.

"How long have you been on the force?" I asked

"5 years, and now, with the increase in violence amongst homeless people in general and the way the city wants to 'sweep' it all under an invisible carpet, well, I decided to try another approach and instead of being heavy handed, I try to relocate the people that the city don't want sleeping on their precious grassy parts."

"Relocate?" I asked.

"Yes, I suggest somewhere else that they should sleep, somewhere I don't have to kick them out of, or I try to also take them to a shelter, knowing the chances of getting a bed at this hour is slim, but trying to assist in any way I can."

Well, this was a first, a cop who was trying harder than most, and trying also to get people off these streets and into shelter. I was impressed. I had his name by now, and we were becoming fast buddies, but I promised him that no matter what happened, I would keep his name out of the book, when and IF I published it.

This officer was a gem amongst rocks. The rocks being in the majority of course.

After an hour or maybe a little longer, sitting chatting, he asked me if I'd like to go to a shelter and he'd use his influence to get me a bed for the remainder of the night. I agreed, and off we went, driving slowly towards the center of town, and back towards the possibility of a somewhat comfy bunk, which was better than the grass bank I'd just left.

No Beach Party

On a carpet of stones, they sat and watched
Admiring huge waves spraying their life's work
Splattering salt across wounded hearts
Fearing nothing other than the end of their journey
Content to be swallowed by the ocean from where they arrived

Gathered in a circle, this was no beach party
Holding hands for warmth and comfort
Feeding only on scenery that had changed so little
Unable to make haste for better times
Rooted to a spot where life seemed never to vary

Eyes scanning a darkening horizon in tandem
Looking out for their savior, praying for rescue
Burning a candle at either end in hope of recognition
Saddened greatly as life passes by on all sides
Ignoring a plight recognized only on days of conscience

An ebbing tide moves closer to completion
Destroying this haven as time moves rapidly forward
Leaving little other than rocks from a distant past
Caring not about their future in continual limbo
Washed up in a life of bitterness and discomfort

My new best friend in life, the cop, was truly a life saver. Not only did he get me a bed, the shelter he took me to was like a palace in comparison to the one I'd stayed in the night before. Within minutes of my head touching the dirty mattress on the bunk bed I'd sneaked into, I was out of it, and sleeping soundly. When I'd arrived everyone else in this shelter was asleep, it was, after all, around 1 AM. When I awoke, jostled out of a slumber by the noise of 50 or more bodies waking up, packing up their belongings, getting ready to walk the streets again, I was startled to find out that it was past 7AM. 6 hours of solid sleep had done wonders for my spirit and given me new life for the day ahead. Again, I realized very quickly that I was only doing this for a week and that everyone else around me had to do this every day. It was so hard to comprehend, thinking always that these people could just march back to their homes and resume a normal existence, just like I was going to do. Unfortunately, that was never the case. These people were stuck, and no one appreciated their plight more than I did at that point. With a little coaxing, and some very sore feet and legs, I got out of bed and made my way to the washroom, standing in line and waiting my turn to get cleaned up. I was offered a simple cold cereal breakfast; I made my way to the front of the building to see if I could find someone in charge and try to 'book' another stay for that night.

Obviously, you cannot book a bed as such, but with my accent and my ability to charm, I thought that perhaps if I could find the right person, explain to them what I was doing, some sympathetic vibes might just come my way and for the remaining three nights, I could return to this place, if that was at all possible. When in doubt, never be frightened to try anything that might work. My only reticence was taking a bed away from someone who really needed it, but having arrived at 1 Am, being given a bunk and then waking up to find they had several bunks still empty; my hesitation didn't last too long. I found the Big Boss, a guy named Stevie.

Stevie, (name changed for obvious reasons), was a very funny guy. He and I hit it off immediately and he'd already been briefed by the night staff, who'd told him I was a friend of Mr. Plod, the policemen and that my intentions were to write a book and donate it's proceeds to shelters or charities like his.

"You're quite the character" he said, as he sheepishly pulled out a bunch of papers, papers that, by their volume and size, spelled more than just a couple of hours work.

"You got to do these every day?" I asked, pointing at the pile.

"Yep. We need to account for every bed and every meal. We're a charity after all and nothing is easy. The government make it difficult for us to run a smooth ship"

I don't know if that's still the case, remembering it's now 14 years since I had this meeting.

He continued.

"Tell me about your book."

And so, I did, and Stevie, if you're reading it, you'll know who you are and even to this day, I thank you for all you did for me that week.

As we were chatting, there was a commotion outside his office, and it sounded like someone or perhaps more than just one, had started a fight. Stevie jumped up and ran to his door, opening it just as a full-blown punch was thrown by this monster of a man, towards a woman, who was half his height and a quarter of his weight. He missed. She kicked him quickly in his testicles, an impressive karate style kick, which landed plum in this guy's nether regions. He hit the deck and she jumped on top of him, fists swinging. She looked like a windmill as her arms rotated and her fists landed on the man's face. There were soon three people, all staff members from the shelter, pulling this woman off the man, who by now was puking his guts up after the kick he'd taken to his 'balls'. The fight was soon over, the lady, a clear winner, and the guy, carted off to wherever they took the losers of these random contests. Probably the front door, where he'd be ejected. He'd started the fight, but she'd ended it. She was also banished into the outside world, and told that if she wanted to come back to the shelter, that night, she'd need to ensure better behavior, or else!

Stevie, sweat pouring down his exasperated face, came back into the room where I was still seated, pulled out the paperwork again, and began chatting away as if nothing had ever happened.

"Another great day in homeless paradise!" he said.

"Happens a lot then?" I asked.

"Every day, and sometimes twice."

"Mental health issues?"

"That and more. These people are so territorial and it doesn't take much to set them off like that. They trust no one, not even their so-called friends, and they trust us, the staff, even less."

I sat for over an hour discussing the work that Stevie and his staff did in this shelter and I came away with the opinion that no matter how hard they tried, how much good they did, how patient and sympathetic they were to all of those who chose to stay with them, they would always remain the enemy in the eyes of those they served. The reason for this? Trust. Homelessness breeds contempt on many levels, and at this level, the level of those who share their lives with those who don't have a normal life, it's very difficult to find a compromise and level of respect that can be transmitted between both without some kind of mistrust and intolerance. It's hard being on either side of this fence, obviously harder on the homeless side, but in general, the lack of empathy on either side was, at that time, there for all to see.

Stevie and I chit-chatted for another hour or so, after which he invited me to spend a day shadowing him at the shelter, offering me the chance to see how things really worked and how difficult his task was to keep the place going and his and the rest of his staff's sanity in check. Since I had no other plans for the day and since the offer and comfort of a space indoors plus the possibility of a decent bed for another night seemed too good to pass up, I agreed.

Forgotten But Never Lost

Left for dead on a street filled with people
Crumpled in a heap of living dirt
Trampled on by stares that could kill more than just one
Screaming silently amongst cobbles called home
Forgotten but never lost as yet another dream passes by
Feeling wanted by fantasy, perhaps ready to come true
Watching closely those who have already succeeded
Joining them, more than just an ingrained passion
Deserted once to often on this quest for recognition

With dirt in each eye as a reminder of what is
Repressed by a soul that has been murdered more than once
Finding from within, happiness in its saddest form
Gazing towards a sunset that cannot yet be seen
Pleasured with the knowledge of many more yet to come
Faint hope now streaming rigorously like blood
Pumped around a body, about to surrender
Giving life to a heart that already died a hundred times before

It takes a lot to keep a shelter going, not just cash, mainly donations and government funding, but people, good people, all with patience, understanding, a sense of humor, and a desire to help out, for much less money than they could probably get elsewhere. There are councilors, cooks, managers, cleaners, and many volunteers too. It's just not as simple as opening a building with some bunk beds and a kitchen. The sanitization process alone, a daily occurrence inside all shelters, ridding the place of lice, vermin, dirt, and so much discarded trash, is in itself, a fulltime job. Government regulations, local authorities, donor requirements, all play their part too, and frankly, it's more red tape than is probably necessary, but this is America, and one wrong move? It's so litigious. The nation on a whole is of course that way, which is very unfortunate on so many levels.

There are several documented law suits across the United States where homeless people have sued establishments such as shelters and restaurants for giving them food that led to food poisoning or other illness. Yes, crazy times are often made even crazier by those who just want to take advantage of their miserable situation by making it even more miserable for those who are trying hard to help them. Regulation, therefore, is a priority at every shelter and now, unfortunately, every food bank, restaurant and café, and even fast-food stores. Based on the fact, and again, this is all very visible if you'd like to research it, that anyone can sue anyone else for anything, especially in America, Stevie was clear in his concise description of the inner workings of this shelter, how much of a stickler they had become for adhering to the law and never taking a chance with even the slightest variation of their own standards, rules and regulations that could create legal issues further down the road.

It's encouraging to note however that even with all the difficulties in this regulatory minefield, there are still willing participants helping those who are less fortunate than ourselves. These people are often overlooked when praise is being handed out by political proponents of a system that is systemically broken. These people are ALWAYS overlooked by the majority of transients who see them day in and day out. I have witnessed this personally on many occasions when I've been present in my voluntary roles in various shelters over the years. There's a tendency to take all the staff who dedicate their day in helping homeless people, for granted, by the people they are there to assist. It's never easy and it's a situation, again, because of our federal government's defunding of mental health programs over the years, that is now out of control and getting worse by the year.

Stevie invited me to chat with anyone in the shelter I thought might make for interesting conversation for my book. I asked him if I could shower first and then if he didn't mind making the introductions. He agreed. I went to wash, cleaned up as best I could and then we began. First stop, the kitchen.

Spotless, from top to bottom, washed twice a day by staff, boarders and volunteers. The kitchen was being run by one head chef, a great guy called Peter, and he worked from 7 Am to 6 PM every day, when another man called Joel would take over. Peter though was regarded as the head chef. His staff, three ladies, all Filipina's, assisted both men and helped cook side dishes on occasion. The whole system was regimented from beginning to end. Food came in from food banks, after Peter had approved their 'purchase.' After it arrived at the shelter, it was stored inside a giant walk-in freezer, which held enough food to last over 3 weeks. The freezer had the proteins and deserts, the pantry, which was situated towards the rear of the kitchen, stored all fruits and veggies and breads and other items like spices, although the spice rack was very basic in content. There was no fancy cooking here, just plain basic essentials, enough to keep a homeless person's belly full for a day or two. Massive, restaurant sized gas burners and three huge ovens, cooked the food. Peter suggested the weekly menu, according to whatever food donations were available and dinner, the only real meal that was cooked daily, would be prepared from 3 PM until serving time at 5. Breakfast was often offered to regulars, but that consisted only of cereal and coffee. No eggs or bacon or other hot food was offered. Peter was no amateur chef by the way. He'd been restaurant trained and was doing this job at the shelter for a very good reason. An accident in his late 20's had sent his whole world into a spiral and he'd ended up on the streets homeless. After some good fortune, meeting people who cared, people who understood his plight, he'd managed, eventually, to get himself back up on his own two feet and decided there and then to dedicate the next ten years of his life to helping other homeless people. He'd interviewed for the job at this shelter, been the best candidate by far and now, 16 years later, was still ensconced in his pledge to be there for those who he once was. He'd never forgotten where he'd come from and now, he swore he was never going back and that he's do everything in his power to make sure other's just like him had the same opportunities. He told me that to date, he'd managed to get over 25 homeless people he'd met at the shelter, into employment, and therefore off the streets of San Francisco. That, I thought, was a miracle indeed.

It seemed that everyone in this place had some form of connection to either being homeless or knowing someone who'd been homeless. The more I chatted, the stronger the connection to a previous homeless experience and present employment circumstance, became clear.

At the front of the shelter, where the entrance was located and where all the lines would form for entry each day, there was a group of offices, mostly occupied by mental health experts, although I use that term loosely, and some of the admin staff, who, with support of donations and government grants, managed to work full-time for very little financial compensation. Most of the staff, exclusive of the therapists, were ex-homeless and had a vast experience of dealing with those people who sought shelter every night. They knew how to speak with them, how to treat them and how to give them back some of their self-respect, albeit in a manner that was often unrewarding and ignored.

I found it extremely interesting that each food delivery was checked, double checked and then stored or refrigerated. The complex manner in which inventory was collated, suggested that theft was kept to a minimum, although, after further discussion with some of the employees, I wasn't too sure my summation of that fact was correct. I kind of think that some of the food deliveries would go AWOL, and end up in places or with people who really could afford to buy their own food. But, in the end, the majority won out and 95% of what came in and was cooked, definitely went to the cause it was meant to be for.

I spent that whole day just rummaging around, listening, chatting, discussing, learning what it was like to either live in a shelter, work in a shelter or just visit a shelter, all of which, I have to say, was an education.

My education was certainly enhanced when the crowd began to arrive around 3 PM, lining up in an orderly fashion outside, ready and waiting to be fed, bathed and bedded. I was again making haste to grab my bed, my place in the line for dinner and my ticket to more stories of gloom and doom, mainly gloom, from the lips of those who had no place to go but around in circles. Walk, beg, line up, eat, sleep, repeat.

Street Party

Forty, he thought but he didn't believe
Loneliness had surpassed time in this awful predicament
Sitting cross legged awaiting his gift
A present from heaven should God smile kindly
Celebration and then gratification would follow
Making life easier for just one fleeting moment

Deeply resentful of those last twenty three years
Unable to call this day his own since youth had robbed him of self esteem
Setting out in a life filled by prospect
Resigned now to death in this gutter of discontent
Wishing for nothing other than that well known tune
Sung in harmony for the first time in many moons

Gloat, they all seemed to gloat as they passed him by
Unknowingly smug in their fine suits and ties
Jealously was a fundamental problem to an unrecognizable face
Seeking cake and perhaps another drink just to toast this occasion
Being left with nothing other than coppers for a cheap meal
Desperate in more ways than one for a shake of his worn hands

Noticing the date on the papers that would become his bed
Confirming that, yes, today was his day
Suddenly uplifted as those notes hit the bottom of his can
Smiling upwards towards that saint who just walked into an invisible future
Generosity allowing for a surprising street party
Joined only by a guest list of undesirables who had become so called friends

Picking up the pieces of his celebratory day in submission
Unwilling to admit that failure had come too easily
Feeling sorry for his lonely soul and broken heart
Knowing that forty should have been his swansong and not his obituary
Deciding quickly that there had to be someone who was less fortunate than he
Unable to find that someone as another lonely birthday ended in the same
place it had begun.

With a bump, a very large fat man hit the deck. His tray, which was filled with his food for the night, dished out royally by one or two of the regular volunteers this shelter boasted, released in midair, spilling its contents all over two other men, sitting innocently at a table enjoying their chicken dinners. Chaos ensued.

I've watched a lot of people fight over the years, mainly on TV or in movies, but when you watch a fight in the flesh, up close and personal, there's a kind of surreal madness about it that makes one wonder what the heck the participants were thinking of, before getting involved in such a fracas?

This fight was no exception. It had clearly been an accident, an accident perhaps just waiting to happen, but an accident all the same.

Fat man had mis-stepped, not too difficult to imagine when you're walking through throngs of people all desperate to eat and all rushing to find a place to sit with their plates filled to brimming with the only real food, they'd seen that day. Just imagine, you've not eaten for 24 hours, you've stood in line for an hour or more, smelling the aroma of what to you, is the best food ever, you eventually are handed a tray, then a plate filled with delicious hot food, some bread and a desert too, and the only thing left on your mind is, 'get my butt on a seat and gorge this food down quickly before someone else does it for me'. Law of the jungle says, its mine, unless I fuck up and then, well, then it's a free-for-all. Fat man, in his rush to sit down, had forgotten that other people were going to be in his path, and with his tongue and belly larger than his ability to apply a common-sense approach to his journey towards a table, he'd tripped on a pair of outstretched legs, gone flying towards a wall and lost his food in a skirmish of predators, all ready and willing to pick up and devour his scraps. Before his legs had hit the floor, 20 people were grabbing his meal and eating it like it was about to magically vanish. Whoosh! All gone. Fat man, now on the floor, a large welt appearing on his face from where it hit the wall he'd crashed into, wasn't taking this lying down, (excuse the pun), and with a deep inhalation of his new-found exasperation, he tried getting up quickly, unfortunately forgetting that his 250lb frame couldn't move like the gazelle he believed he could be.

A comedy on two legs is how I'd describe his attempts to raise his huge frame and then go after the 20 or so who were in the process of eating his meal. Two staff members tried to calm him down, telling him not to get to upset and that they would provide him another meal, and get him help to clean his wound. He wasn't having it though and without warning he lunged at one of his predators, hitting him squarely in his face with a right hook and breaking his nose. Blood spurted from this new wound, and fat man, now triumphant, looked around the room to pursue more victims, ready and willing to dish out the very same punishment to them as he had to the guy whose nose he'd just broken. It became a free-for-all, 20 to 30 bodies in a rugby-like scrum. No winners, no losers, just carnage without the blood and guts. Comedy like and very verbal, as punches missed, karate kicks went wide of their mark and head butts, well, let's just say that there were going to be some very sore necks from all the back and forth without any direct contact. Hilarious, but sad, and all over within 2 minutes. I wish I could have recoded it on video or at least been able to sketch it. It would have made for a very funny newspaper cartoon the following morning. Caption, "How many homeless people does it take to devour a plate full of food?"

Oh dear, what a mess that was, what a complete mess. Sorted out eventually, we all got back to eating, except for fat man, shamed and bloodied, then exiled to his 'special' corner, where, after he'd finished his meal, was escorted to his 'special' resting place, never to be seen again that evening.

Bedtime soon arrived and although the shelter had a certain 'buzz' about it after the fight earlier that evening, I settled into another bunk in the hope that another good night's sleep would bring about a very productive day 5, meaning all I had to do was move around the city for 2 more days and then it would be all over for me. Or would it really just be starting? My ambitions had certainly been cemented by my experiences so far and the urge to write this book, although it took me many years more to actually complete that task, had been peaked by everything I'd seen and done, all the people, characters I'd met, and the need to resolve this homeless crisis once and for all.

Head down, sweater as a pillow once again, and it was lights out to another strange day.

Theatre of Death

A pale blue moon flickers intermittently behind passing clouds
Creating a strobe light on the dance floor of death
A theatre filled by an unwanted audience
Waiting anxiously each night for a rousing finale
Signaling release from this life of non-existence

Bewilderment alongside resignation consuming each participant
Wrapped up inside degradation and continual abuse
Drawn towards this show that never ends
Finding safety amongst fellow connoisseurs and aficionados
Bunking down between dampness and dirt to gain a better view

Through long dark hours of incessant unseen terror
Huddled together in readiness for the unexpected
Loners, finding solace between their fix
Praying that on this night they will again have much luck
Hoping for, but not welcoming the sight of another miserable dawn

With begging bowls hidden beneath a needless bounty of unsavory purchase
Feasting upon stories of mistreatment and ignorance
Relentless in pursuit of an exit back towards broken dreams
Unable to eject the stigma carried upon their backs through the longest days
Knowing this may be the last shining star they will ever gaze upon

Lights out as toxicity overwhelms an ability to remain coherent
Steadfast, they lock arms inside a circle of desperation
Shaking and shivering but not from the cold air which surrounds them
Ready and waiting for the arrival of better times
Living in fear amongst friends in an underground society of abandoned souls

I awoke at 4 am, and something smelled bad, really bad. That smell had obviously torn me away from this great dream I was having, although quite what that dream was, I will never know.

My nose is like a bloodhound's nose. I can smell anything from 500 ft, guess what it is, and get it right every time. This time, 5 feet was enough. Some man, about two bunks to my left, had so obviously shit himself while he was asleep, and now as he lay there submerged in his own poop, snoring and quite unaware of his dream induced bowel movement, the stench his ablutions had created was one of the worst smells my poor nose had ever had to endure. The stench was so bad, I believed I was going to throw up. I jumped out of bed, grabbed my gear and headed to the bathroom, where, when I arrived still half asleep, I picked a stall, shut the door and sat. I was gasping for breath, honestly, no exaggeration, I was gasping! It took me an hour to come out of that stall, having heard the commotion in the bunkroom as the staff tried to wake this guy and clean him up. Poos sods, they not only worked the night shift, but they had the most unpleasant tasks sometimes, and I felt for them. When I thought it was safe to go back and lie down on my bunk again, I gingerly stepped back into the room only to be met with the lingering residue of a smell that I believed could have been used effectively in biological warfare. The culprit had been removed, cleaned up, and then taken to a different room for medical evaluation. Yes, they have limited medical assistance at these shelters, but all this guy needed, in my humble opinion, was a cork up his ass and an education on what not to eat. He wasn't an old guy, so don't get me wrong, he had no obvious medical issues that I could tell of, but something had gone right through him and after the event, all I could think of was drug abuse. For some reason, and don't ask me why, drugs along with lack of nutrition and germ-infested streets made for a lifestyle, again, in my opinion, that could lead to accidents such as the one I'd just witnessed. I decided to make it my task for that day to investigate further.

I'd told Stevie that I would assist with something, anything, in the shelter, just to pay him back for the goodness he'd shown to me by setting me up with a bunk for the rest of my days as a homeless impersonator. Stevie had suggested I help clean the bathrooms and the kitchen, and I gladly agreed. At least it would keep me busy and it would mean that for a few hours I wouldn't need to worry about walking around San Francisco's streets looking for something to occupy those endless hours of boredom. I always believed research as a writer might be interesting. I suppose authors like Grisham and Clancy and their likes, have glamorous written all over their novels and so walking the streets of Moscow or Savanah finding material for their next book might be quite enjoyable. And then there's me. Slogging away as a homeless impersonator, digging for gold in garbage cans, wearing used smelly old clothing, sleeping on streets and on bunk beds with hundreds of others. All I could think about was, "why didn't I write successful crime thrillers, or even Harry Potter books??" What a choice I'd made, hopefully a choice that one day would be rewarded, not personally to me, but to those I was there to write about. Getting hundreds out of poverty and off the streets would be just amazing, but to get hundreds of thousands into their own homes? Ambitious perhaps, but in my opinion, very doable. Just thinking of the children gave me the inspiration I required to see this venture through to its inevitable ending. Those poor kids, and average age of 9!! So sad.

Cleaning up shit therefore meant very little in the grand scheme of things.

My assistance on that particular morning was welcomed and much appreciated. I began in the bathrooms, cleaning and scrubbing all of the grime and shit out of every inch of tile. It was absolutely disgusting and honestly one of the worst things I'd even done in my life. And the smell?? It reeked of death, and that's the only way I could describe it. I cannot understand how so many Jews coped in the concentration camps, cleaning up dead bodies after they'd been gassed. That must have been like living in Hell, and from what I've read on the subject of the Holocaust, maybe worse than any Hell we can ever imagine. This task I'd begun, seemed to go on for hours. An endless, mindless task, propelled by a desire to exit this area as soon as was humanly possible. After I was done, and by the way, there were three of us cleaning, not just me, I begged for a shower and the smell of fresh bread or lemons or freshly cut grass, just to reverse the sensation of the smell from the toilets, now ingrained inside my brain. I believe it took about a week to really get past the feeling of wanting to puke every time I thought about what I'd been doing, but eventually, the trauma, if I can put it that way, evaporated and although still fresh in my mind today, my ability to compartmentalize the sensation of wanting to puke has now overwhelmingly succeeded my inabilities to do so on that particular day.

I was moved into the kitchen, and the cleaning began again, only this time the odor of rotting food was a much nicer smell that the bathrooms. We cleaned all morning and then I asked Stevie if I might help with something else. He declined my offer, stating it would be better for me to exit the shelter and rejoin all of the other homeless people around the city, just in case suspicion was ever pointed towards my sudden involvement inside that shelter. I wanted to try and retain my cover for as long as possible and knew really were only 2 more nights to go and one and a half days. My intentions were to go home early morning on day 7, leaving all of this behind and then turning my experiences into words as soon as possible. As you now know, that didn't happen, and it's taken 14 years and a lot more adventures to come to terms with my journey and improve my ability to relate my story in words that are hopefully eloquent and entertaining.

Funny Sign

This was his corner, a prized possession
Paradise of sorts, though not picture perfect
Standing alone, stripped of all dignity
Able to offer up a fake smile, but only just
Reduced to insignificance by circumstance

Still carrying a sense of humor
Abused by the minute, though not physically
His sign, a funny sign, telling the truth
Asking politely, never begging
Condemned to hiding behind simple words

An occasional saint stops to chat
Sometimes donating towards his habit
Knowing the truth and caring little for excuses
Ridding his conscience of just a little guilt
Marching onwards toward future prosperity

And so, stuck in his rut, he rarely moves
Dawn to dusk, pleading for more
Feeding addiction, ingrained for many years
Listed numerically on his board
There for the world to laugh at, there for a reason

The sun was out and it was warmer than usual when I left the shelter. I planned to sleep there again that night and also again the following night and Stevie had promised to reserve me a bed in full payment for helping to clean the place. I assured him I would assist again the next morning, but he insisted that my volunteer work that day was quite sufficient and that my two further nights stays were well-deserved.

It turned out that, on this particular afternoon, tourists seem to be everywhere, and bearing in mind my previous success's panhandling, I decided to see how much money I could make in the 5 or so hours I had until my return to the shelter for dinner came around. I also decided that every penny I made would be given away to people I met when I went back for my dinner and my bunk-bed. In my own mind, this was now a competition. I'd been given that $100 from the Israeli couple, now I had to challenge myself to go one better and try to reach $200, knowing that most people would normally give out $1 and not $100 at a time. This was going to be a mammoth task, but I got into it right away as I approached this woman who it turned out was Russian. My spiel went something like this,

"Hi young lady" I said, as she tried to avoid me, and turned her head the other way as her feet just kept on walking.

"Please don't walk away, I am quite friendly, I promise."

She stopped and looked at me, giving me the once over from top to bottom and then deciding it was time to pass and move on. I could tell from her eyes that she wasn't having any of my spiel, and so without waiting, I continued.

"You speak English, right? Yes, I'm sure you do. Listen, I am very familiar with this city and if you'd like to know where you should go today, without wasting time just walking around, I am happy not only to be your guide, but if you don't like the look of me, and yes, I know I am very badly dressed, then for a small fee, I can suggest where you need to go." Again, after a brief hesitation, she walked on and didn't give me a second glance. In fact, I could sense that she'd stuck her nose in the air to suggest 'who the fuck was that and why did I even bother to stop and listen.'

Oh well, one down, and never shy of a challenge, I perused the crowd and tried again. Next guy coming up seemed like an American, but I wasn't 100% convinced of that just yet.

"Sir" I began,"are you interested in hearing some tourist tips from a Scot who is homeless and in need of cash to survive?"

He stopped, and this time I knew I'd hooked one.

"You're Scottish?" he said, with a broad southern US accent.

"Tennessee?" I asked

"How'd you know" he replied, and as he did so, his wife and kids came up behind us and joined him. His wife, unfortunately, wasn't so curious.

"Honey, what are you doing?" she questioned

"This guys from Scotland and he's homeless but willing to help us out with some ideas on places to visit today" the man said, as he grabbed his wife's hand.

She kind of pulled away from him, placing her arm around her kids as if trying to protect them from some kind of onslaught. The man, who by now was definitely interested in what I had to say, was less cautious and more apt to having a discussion with me.

"Where should we go? We asked the hotel and they gave us a list, but what would you do if you were me and had the three of them to please all day?" he asked, as he pointed to his wife and kids.

"Other than the usual suspects, the Golden Gate Bridge and Alcatraz and the Wharf," I began, "in my humble opinion, I would take the kids and do a tour of AT&T Park"

As I said this, I looked at the young boy, probably around 14 years of age, and I asked him, "do you like baseball?"

He nodded in the affirmative.

"I took my daughter there once. She loves the Giants, and we both loved the tour, even though I'm not really into baseball. It's fun and it's educational, and I think that you'd all really like it."

He paused and thought for a moment. "How long have you been homeless?"

"About 4 days" I told him, which was completely true.

"Why are there so many homeless people here in this city? Quite honestly, it's scary and at times we wonder why we even bothered to come here." "I can assure you, most of them are very nice and most of them will not bother you, and the one's that aren't are to be avoided like the plague. This city is now underwater with homeless people and it's bringing the city to its knees." "You're very knowledgeable" he said.

"Well, I've lived in the area for many years, so I should be. Anyway, I don't want to take up any more of your time, so please have a wonderful day and enjoy whatever you are going to do."

"Dad" said the boy, "can we do the stadium tour please?"

The dad agreed and just as I was departing, thinking I'd done something nice for someone and not expecting anything other than a thank you, the man pulled out a $20 from his pocket and thrust it into my hand.

"Thanks so much. Appreciate you." He said, and as he did, they all walked off into the thronging crowds that seemed to be making their way to no place in particular, although all with a certain unknown purpose.

The smell of my disgusting clothing was beginning to get to me, and believe me, with my bloodhound nose, that was troubling. I really needed a change, and knowing I could walk into any store I wanted, buy what I wanted, anytime I wanted, was kind of driving me nuts. Even though I had no money with me, other than what I'd panhandled, the mere thought of taking that cash and walking into Macy's, buying a new sweater and walking out, just to relieve the odor coming from my person, was almost too much to pass up. However, I stuck with my plan, knowing I had less than 48 hours to go and I plodded on towards my next destination.

The tram in San Francisco is a very popular tourist attraction, in fact, it's probably number 2 in popularity after the Golden Gate bridge. There's always a line to get on, a line that sometimes can take over an hour to wade through. There are two very popular terminus points, one is at the Ghirardelli square end and the other is at Market St, some 4 miles over the top of some very steep hills. As I was close to Market St, I walked towards the line of tourists I knew would be impatiently standing and waiting for their turn to board the tram car, hoping I might make a few bucks from the foreigners I expected to find there. I myself had stood in this line several times, and I knew that a visit from a persistent, unwelcome homeless person, was not something any of these people wanted to see or listen to. I had to come up with something that might entertain them, something they would appreciate and something that might give my donation target a realistic chance of succeeding. I'd seen homeless people trying their best to antagonize those lines of waiting tram-goers, I'd also seen other street people, entertainers of sorts, perform guitar solos, statuesque feats that were mind-boggling, bagpipe players, mono-cyclists, and so whatever it was I decided to do, it had to be different, unusual or just downright unimaginable, otherwise I'd just be seen as one of many and not an original. My mind went into overdrive as I covered the 6 or so blocks from where I was to where I wanted to be. My issues were as follows. I looked homeless, I was homeless, I couldn't dance, sing, play an instrument, but, and it was a huge but, I did have a great sense of humor and could tell jokes on demand. I knew jokes about everyone and everything, and at that point in my walk towards this tram line, I decided that's what I would be, the homeless comedian. Give me $10 and I will tell you a joke, or better still, I will tell a joke about any subject you want and if you like it, you give me a donation in any amount you like?

Yep, the plan was formulating nicely in my head, my only concern? Would it work and would I have the balls to see it through? The answers to both questions were unknown, but with less than 3 blocks to go, my plan was the only plan I had at that moment in time and depending on the length of the line when I arrived and the number of other entertainers and beggars that were around, it seemed like this was my only option.

I arrived, nervous and troubled by the number of other panhandlers who were circling the waiting crowd.

The attention span of a child is negligible, and the attention span of a child who's been waiting in line to get on a tram for an hour or more, is nonexistent. They hate being dragged around by their parents, they hate the fact that it's hot and sunny and that there is no shade to shelter under, and lastly, they can't stand the fact they are surrounded by lunatics and smelly people who want only to beg, steal or borrow from their parents. Most of them have this attitude that says, "get me out of here and do it now!' I knew this and I also knew that if I could make them laugh, I'd have a chance of at least making a few bucks from entertaining those children during their period of boredom. It was time to perform.

At the top of my lungs, "OK ladies and gentlemen, and all you bored kids waiting in this line to take the tram, it's time to laugh. I am Alan, the homeless comedian, here to entertain you and make your time standing in this line pass quickly and with a certain amount of laughter."

As I shouted this, the other guys who were also entertainers, trying hard to get every dollar they could from a line that hardly moved, took a little step back and looked at me as if they were about to kill me. I had two choices, carry on, or run fast. I stayed.

"What's the best time to go to the dentist?" I asked this little girl, who was about 3 ft tall, wearing a Disney princess dress and had her thumb in her mouth. She must have been 4 or 5.

She shrugged her shoulders as if to say "I don't know" but her mouth remained closed around her thumb and she refused to answer. I looked at her parents, and they laughed, I looked back at her and she remained coy, and so, with the punch line looming, I stepped forward to deliver it with some vigor and some cheer, when suddenly, out of nowhere, I was shoved in the back and pushed to the ground. I hadn't seen it coming, but I sure felt it, with my hands outstretched in a protective mode as my head fell towards the concrete sidewalk. The standing tram crowd gasped. One lady shrieked.

The little girl stepped back and the thud that I felt on my knees as my legs hit the ground, was shattering. I spun around quickly to see what had happened and as I did so, I noticed that there were two sets of legs standing over me. My face was facing into the sun and it was hard to see exactly who the legs belonged to, but it wasn't long before their features were revealed and our confrontation began. This, I could tell, was going to be an easy fix.

Two old homeless guys, both drunk and hardly able to stand on their own two feet were the culprits and my aggressors. The crowd by now was in standby mode, waiting anxiously to see how this little contretemps would play out, and the little girl I'd been about to deliver my punchline to was now on her tram with the rest of her family, and headed out to the wharf.

I jumped up, I went up to the guy on the left of me, with my face touching his face, and I could feel his fear. The other guy had backed off slightly, and was kind of retreating, but this one, the first one I'd challenged, well, he was standing his ground.

"What the fuck is your problem asshole?" I asked.

And then, the funniest thing happened. He began to speak, but I had no idea what was coming out of his mouth. It was complete drunken gobbledygook. Slurring strange words, spitting out unheard of expletives and trying as hard as he could to remain standing in an upright position, alcohol fueling whatever state this man was in. Before he'd gone too far with this verbal onslaught, he suddenly stopped, looked around for the other guy, who was obviously his back up, and when he realized the man had vanished into the crowd, he looked again at me and threw a punch, which missed me by a good 12 inches, but its momentum spun drunk man around and floored him as it came all the way round his body and smacked him in his own mouth. It was hilarious and it was hard not to stop laughing, laughter which I could now hear coming from many who were standing in line for the next tram.

"And that, ladies and gentlemen, is how not to throw a punch" I shouted. More laughter. "In fact, I would love to show you all the correct way to flatten an aggressor, the likes of which you have all seen since you arrived in this city, but I fear that if I just touched this drunken lout, he'd collapse like the pack of cards he is. All he needs is yet another drink, and he's hoping one or two of you will fuel his impossible habit. But we all know better than to do that, don't we?" I shouted. Heads nodding in the affirmative could be seen all the way up the tram line. I continued. "Instead of fueling this man's habit, let's be generous, let's have a collection for his mental wellbeing in the hope that someone somewhere will assist this man in getting out of the homeless poverty in which he unfortunately finds himself, and let's hope that one day, his words can be understood and his demand for alcohol of any kind can be rescinded."

I received a round of applause from about 200 standing tourists, all of whom were now transfixed to this scene. I hadn't a clue where all those words had come from, but I didn't care. Everyone seemed to be digging deep into their pockets and bringing out dollar bills, ready and willing to hand them over to me. The drunk guy had collapsed in a heap next to my feet, and passed out. He hadn't a clue what was happening around him. I decided to collect my 'winnings' from all of the outstretched hands, thanking each and every one of them, as I pocketed almost $35 from their generosity.

"Way to go."

"You got him."

"What an asshole."

Just some of the comments I heard as I quietly put the cash in my pocket and made my way to a different spot, a spot which hopefully would be safer and just as generous. As for drunk guy? Well, I have no idea what happened to him, but just before I left, I put $5 in one of his coat pockets, thanking him sincerely for making it easier for me and for not having to perform as a comedian.

Delectable Drunk

His passion was women, often and many
Driven by the never-ending chase
Insatiable desires so rampant
Multiple opportunities fueling his fire
Unlimited vocabulary his secret weapon

His elixir was Port wine
Enticing red liquid, poison for his soul
Tea totaling perfectionist turned inebriated womanizer
One glass set fire to his loins
Degenerating conversation with comedic form

A delectable drunk, loved by the world
Expectations rarely exhausted
Leading one after another to sexual bliss
Chastised by those whom he had loved too much
Breaking hearts whilst consuming banter

They fell, like the shots he could drink
One after another, so repetitive
Enjoyment only in the climax
The bottle, like his libido, now empty
Corked again and raring to go another round

Jocular he may seem, as the liquid ran dry
Pleasantly aggressive as vulgarity spewed forth
Insecurities from his past wreaking havoc with his future
Drowned immediately as infatuations became reality
She laughed uncontrollably as his cork popped once more

The rest of that short afternoon was incredibly boring. Walking, sitting, walking again and just thinking about what it would be like to be a homeless person for the rest of my life. Believe me when I tell you, it's not something I would ever want to do again, not even for a short period of time. It's desperate, it's saddening, it's horribly frightening, and it's so lonely. There's just nobody to talk to, to discuss the latest news, sports, home life, just nobody. Those who do chat to you are gone within moments, and you rarely, if ever, see them again. I suppose if I was living on the city's streets permanently, things would be different and I would meet the same people now and then, but honestly, these people are often so drugged up, or so angry with society, it's just not worth beginning any kind of conversation with any of them. Eventually a conversation leads to something unsavory, as had happened to me on several occasions that week and unsavory was something I was simply trying to avoid. When it came down to the facts, I was fortunate, these people were not. They were placed on these streets either by circumstance or by choice, but either way, it was a jungle and survival of the fittest was the only way you could get through each day. The kids? The kids were truly victims, completely undeserving of any of this and unfortunately stuck there because of their parent's plight to get out and back into normality as soon as their circumstances changed. But looking at the kids, and believe me, there are dozens of them, and thinking about their futures? How many of them would escape this world? How many of them would end up leading normal lives? How many would be addicted to some kind of substance abuse or living a life of crime and the big question, the $64,000 question, how many would make it past their 18th birthday alive?

After spending most of that afternoon just hanging around the Market St area, as time passed and my patience grew even thinner, I thought it was time to head back to the shelter and to see if I could assist Stevie and the rest of the team with dinner prep or something else, just to keep me occupied until bedtime. I picked myself up and brushed myself down, I was so dirty, my nose was filled with pollution and city dust, my eyes hurt and my head was spinning, and not in a good way.

This had been one crazy week so far, and only God knew how much crazier it could get.

I entered the shelter, by now, everyone knew me. I walked past the front desk, nodding and smiling to Janet, the lady behind that desk, asking her how her day had been and inquiring as to Stevie's whereabouts? Janet pointed me towards the back door, letting me know that a delivery of food had just arrived and that the team were off-loading the truck. I decided to go and help.

It's quite incredible how much food is donated to food banks and yet, it's never enough. I've stood outside Family Ministry shelters handing out food and until you do this, you do not realize how many people are actually going hungry or just cannot afford to feed their families. It often gets to the point of complete exasperation, especially when you see kids in the back seats of cars that drive in looking for assistance and your heart just breaks for them, knowing that you have enough at home to feed all of them and still have enough left over to feed yourself. There are also those who are going to break the rules, and believe me, I have seen it firsthand. There are people who use and abuse the charity of giving, of course there are, and there always will be. I watched a lady at Albertsons pay with food stamps, or whatever you call them here in America. She had a cart full of goodies, and when she offered the food stamps in lieu of payment, I had never seen that done before. When my turn came to pay, I asked the cashier what the previous woman had paid with and she kindly explained that the lady had been on government assistance. "Ah!" I thought, "makes sense and good for her. Feeding her family."

I paid, walked out the store, and would you believe it, that same lady, the food stamp lady, was unloading her cart into the trunk of her SUV, a BRAND-NEW SUV! A Cadillac, no less. It still had the dealer stickers on it, that's how new it was. Total BS. Paying with food stamps and driving a new car?? Some of the other shelters I've volunteered at have seen cars drive up, people asking for food supplies, but when you actually look inside their car, the kids are all beautifully dressed, have lovely new backpacks and are sporting sneakers that sell for $100 plus! It's such a shame that people buck the system and abuse privilege. There are certainly very poor people who need more than other's and abuse of the system just exacerbates the need for people to donate more, and for more people to take more. It's quite sad and it goes mainly unmonitored. Standing at these places giving away supplies is heartwarming, heartbreaking and can make you become a heartless person, especially when you see and speak to those who should never be in these lines for food in the first place.

One year I volunteered to give out Thanksgiving dinner at a church in San Jose. The crowds were huge, all waiting patiently outside that church for the best meal they would get before Christmas. Volunteers were also aplenty, all with a conscience or a desire to help because they had nothing better to do that day. The line was offered entry and homeless and poor people began walking into the dining hall to be fed. When this began, I couldn't help notice several in line with brand new shoes on, perhaps a not so old coat and some very clean shaved men, who looked like they'd just come out of a health club. Now I know that God says, do not judge, but when you see abuse of privilege, just like that, it's hard to keep one's mouth shut and accept that these so-called poor people are just sponging off a system which is supposedly there for the needy. It used to be easy to tell someone to 'fuck off' if you believed them to be a fraud, but now, all that would do would be create a law suit and unwanted publicity for a charity trying it's best to fulfill a promise. Feed the hungry and not those who just want a free meal. How can we discriminate? Very difficult not to, but impossible to implement that discrimination because you just never know who is real and who is fake. It could be that a man or woman who looks and dresses very nicely has just recently run out of luck and has been relegated to begging for food or money in the days prior to you meeting them. There no possible way to find out the real truth regarding anyone's situation unless you're lucky enough to follow them home and check into every living detail about their life, something that will never happen. In the meantime, these charities just feed those who show up in the hope that an honor system of sorts exists and exists with complete fairness and conscious, which is asking a lot in this day and age. People just take what they can get, when they can get it. If it's free, its good. But don't get me started, it's a wicked enough world without the abusers we have in our society, taking advantage just because they can.

Back to my day at the shelter, and Stevie had seen me coming through the hall towards where their truck was being off-loaded, shouting at me to hurry because they really needed to get this completed and dinner service prepared for the line that was forming outside.

"Glad you're back" he said, 'thought I told you we didn't need you anymore, but I was wrong."

"Happy to help" I said, and I took my coat off ready to shift box after box from the truck to the pantry and freezer. It's amazing what kind of foods are donated. There are all sorts of proteins, but rarely any fish. Weird? Yes, I have rarely if ever seen fish served at any shelter I've volunteered at before. It's always pork, beef or chicken. Must be something to do with the price? Not sure, but hey, I am not involved in the procurement of any of this stuff. There are deserts by the dozen, mainly deserts that are frozen, such as cheesecake, key-lime pies etc. Fruit and veg, often in canned format, is plentiful. Fresh veg, harder to get, but depends on the time of year and the amount the food-bank receives. Bread, many differing kinds, is also plentiful. I read once that the United States discards enough bread each day to fill a 100,000-person stadium, like the Rose Bowl in Pasadena. Unreal wastage, every day!! And then there are all the condiments and spices and oils required to cook all of this food and to turn it into a varying cacophony of exotic of even just normally plain tasting dishes, adding a variety of flavor to all who need to be fed daily. All of these accompanying accoutrements, salt, pepper, seasonings, need to be accounted for when visiting the food-bank to claim the weekly shop for each shelter. There's just so much that goes into taking care of those who cannot take care of themselves, it's mind-blowingly difficult. At one point in my volunteer work in a shelter in San Jose, I recall the chef, Paul, letting me know that their food stock was down to such a bare minimum, that he didn't think he could feed the expected 250 people that would come in that evening, and I also remember him telling me that the food bank was so low on supplies that he didn't believe he'd be able to prepare any food the next day. It's called living on a knife's edge. No donations, no food at the food-bank, no meals for those who have nothing. One cog misses it's turn, and the whole engine comes to a shuddering and immediate halt. We, as a country, have enough for everyone, the issue is, not everyone has the belief that they have enough for those who have nothing.

Happy Thanksgiving

A black refuse bag strung over a shoulder in pain
Carried with dignity toward a church that cares
Smiling in the knowledge that satisfaction is on his horizon
This, the one day where he is certain to feast
Taken care of by the caring
Fed by those who are already full

One hand leading his march to dignity
Brisk steps on an empty stomach
Grimace turned to anticipation
Whistling to the tune of thoughts from a distant past
Happiness, long gone, returned just for this moment
Breathtaking in the eyes of one so neglected

His pursuit of a basic right taking up all his attention
Masked only by the solemn looks he receives from passers by
Mocking this unknown due only to ignorance and wealth
Lacking in respect, oblivious to his challenge
Reeling under the weight of ostentation
Never thinking this could happen to them

On this day in particular, prayers seem so unimportant
Answered in the form of a full belly
Giving much thanks to any who care to listen
Taking time as each morsel is digested in both mind and stomach
Regaining strength to survive yet another winter
Returning back to the streets having had a happier Thanksgiving Day

After emptying the truck, I needed to wash or shower and Stevie allowed me to use the staff bathroom. It was so much cleaner and pleasant than the communal one and I spent a good 20 minutes cleaning up. My last full day and night would be tomorrow, but for now, I was hungry and ready to dish out some of the cash I'd made earlier that afternoon. I trusted myself to find some worthy recipients, hopefully! The line for dinner was small that evening, no doubt some of the regulars were elsewhere, either getting drunk, shooting up, or otherwise engaged. This particular shelter catered for about 300 a night, I reckoned there might be 100 at a push.

More would eventually show up, but my concern was giving to those who were present and not those who might decide to turn up later.

I looked around at the incoming line of poverty and desperation. It was so sad, even at this point in time, after a week on the streets, to consider the options these people had in life. So cruel their misfortune, so incredibly sad their predicament, so unbelievably disgusting that they were to be left like this. I was always told, never give money to a homeless person, buy them food, socks, shoes or clothing. If you give them money, they will blow it on drugs. This is not always the case, but throughout my years of working close to or directly with homeless people, that advice has nearly always rung true. I once wandered from my office in Los Gatos, California, to the downtown area of that city for dinner. I ate Chinese food that night but was given so much on my plate that half of it was boxed up and ready to be taken home for future meals. That's the thing about America, the portions at most restaurants are huge and can feed two or three people at a time. Perhaps if some restraint was put on portion size and the distribution of the portion wealth was divvied out to those less fortunate than ourselves, some of the hunger we see on our streets might be rescinded? Anyway, with my boxed up left overs in hand, I made my way back to my office. On the way, I saw this elderly lady, not for the first time, I had seen her often and sometimes I'd given her money, knowing she was homeless and destitute. On this particular evening, I saw her lying in the street, so I approached, gingerly of course in order not to scare her off, and offered her my Chinese left overs. She stopped what she was doing and looked up at me.

"Would you like this food" I asked, "it's Chinese sweet and sour chicken."

She sat still, pondering her choice and trying hard to make a decision. I knew she had some unknown metal health issues, but I didn't know exactly what was making her so hesitant.

"Is that REAL chicken?" she asked me.

And it was at that point in my life that I came to terms with my passion for trying to resolve homelessness in America and the rest of the world. Her statement, "Is that REAL chicken', had brought me to tears. I don't know why, but it did. I came to a brief but final understanding on how these people take nothing for granted, and even though I knew she had some mental issues, the fact that she was asking me if the chicken was real or fake, drew every breath of air I had inside me and turned it immediately into pity, maybe self-pity. It was my moment to God. Sounds weird, I know, but knowing I could go anywhere at any time and buy chicken or beef or anything else I wanted and never question the price, the fact that if I had leftovers I could eat them, discard them or give them away, the fact that I never had to question anything I did, and yet, there I was, confronted by someone without choice, asking if the chicken was REAL? It threw me a curve ball and it made me realize, as if I hadn't already realized it, that I was certainly one lucky bastard and there but for the grace of God....

'Yes, the chicken is real. Would you like it?" I asked her again.

Of course, she accepted it, taking it gently from my hand, putting it into her Walgreens shopping cart that she pushed up and down Los Gatos high street, and slowly made her way to the little park in the center of town, where, as I watched her sit on the grass, she took the container out, and as she opened the box, smelling its contents, she just admired them. She never ate any of it, and I stayed close by for at least 20 minutes. She just stared at it as if it was a gold bar she'd just found on the street. Her facial expression never changed, dead pan and unmoved, but I could tell from within me that she was overcome with gratitude and mesmerized that she'd been given a life-line into tomorrow, understanding perhaps that a complete stranger had been her daily angel. That woman's face is vividly imprinted in my memory today, and that was more than 25 years ago.

Back at the shelter, bearing in mind I always bought food for those I thought needed it most, I had a decision to make. I had about $120 in my possession and I needed about $15 for train fare to get back to San Jose. I would hide that, just in case no more funding was forthcoming. I thought it best to hand out increments of $5 to some of the people I believed could be most deserving of this cash, but unfortunately, I had some $20's too and Stevie and co had gone home for the evening. Still, I could hand out my $5's and wait for Stevie to change my $20's the following day, right? Only problem, when you begin handing out cash in a homeless shelter, word gets around and suddenly your safety is at risk. Let me explain why.

Lancelot

Arthur sat, at his table, so round
Lancelot by his side, left, and right
Surrounded, not an empty seat in the house
All with daggers, though completely unarmed
Ready, waiting, this fight, already lost
Surrender, a given, taken for granted
Mostly anger, now a certain calm
Resolution in the face of calamity
All noble knights, looking for noble rights
Vagabonds, just looking for pay
A coming together, but not of minds
Distinctly segregated by agenda
Battle, already commenced and over
Result, a tie, a dead heat
No winners and all losers
Breaking up, yet again, to face another day
Hand in hand, on a march to further separation

Money, ah yes, the be all and end all. Can't live without it, and if you have it, try hanging on to is without everyone you know wanting to get their hands on it. Story of life, story of death and the story we all talk about, each day, all day, and don't deny it or I'll call you a liar!

Now, try putting yourself inside the shoes of someone who has nothing. No money, no food, no family, no hope, no nothing! Then try imagining what it would be like to be given something, a glimmer of hope a little gift, a promise of just something, knowing THAT something will increase your chances of survival for just one precious day by 100-fold. Giving, yes, it's one of life's greatest pleasures, unfortunately though, people who give are often abused and harassed into giving even more and the 'takers' of this world know just how to manipulate those givers. As the saying goes, 'give an inch and they take a yard', or something just like that. When deciding who to give to at the shelter, it was imperative to ensure that money was distributed to those who were in dire need as opposed to those who were just needy and also to those who would not be prone to asking for more, a decision, my decision, made even more difficult by my lack of personal knowledge on who any of these possible recipients might be and what their reaction could be if money was freely flying around their presence. Remembering that I was only going to give away $5 bills and remembering also I'd had past experiences giving $100 bills away to similar characters, I kind of let my nose do the leading and if my gut told me to offer up a greenback, I would just do it, in the hope that decision would be correct and without retribution, either physical or verbal.

I took my food from the counter and sat at a table, just like everyone else who came before or after me. Dinner consisted of meatloaf, mashed potatoes, corn and two slices of bread, with a slice of raspberry strudel for dessert. We were all allowed to help ourselves to water, but no other beverage was permitted, for obvious reasons. Although that never really stopped anyone trying to sneak illegal drink into dinner, everyone, without exception was searched before they entered the shelter and any 'contraband' that was found would be confiscated. No alcohol, no drugs and no weapons. This rule being strictly enforced for everyone's safety.

Two young lads sat down next to me. One looked like he was in his late teens and the other maybe early 20's. We got chatting. For the purpose of this book, the older of the two we can call Rob, the younger Bob.

"How's it going?" I asked.

"Terrible" said Bob, without any hesitation. I could tell he was flustered.

"What happened today?" I continued.

"We walked about 15 miles from South San Francisco to here and we tried hard to get a few dollars from some people we met along the way, but we got nothing and arriving here, we're fucking starving, and this," he said pointing at his dinner, "isn't going to fill us up," said Rob.

"How'd you guys end up on the streets and how long you been homeless?" I asked.

"Where are you from?" came the response from Rob.

"Scotland" I replied.

"We left Minnesota a few weeks ago. They offered us a free bus ride down here" Bob began, "we thought California sounded like a great place to hang out. Sunshine and beaches and snow and great looking chicks and the promise of work." He looked at Rob and raised his eyebrows as if to say, how wrong could we have been. He continued chatting.

"We both came through the foster system in Minnesota and we met when we were in our teens. I'm still only 19, he's 20, and we needed to get out and away from all the abuse we received. The city gave us bus tickets to get here, free."

"Wait, you got here free?" I was surprised.

"Yeah, us and about 100 other homeless people. They cleared us out of Minneapolis, just to make it look good and so they could say that they'd cleaned up their streets. They told us the weather in California was much better and we'd have more chance of surviving because their winters were not as brutal as the one's in Minnesota. When they offered us the tickets, we had no hesitation. We were on the run anyway, no job, no place to live and no way to get work," said Rob.

"You were on the run?" I asked, confused and presuming they were criminals of some kind.

"Yes, the foster system kicked us both out at 18, we had no families, we'd become friends and we both wanted to make something of our lives, but you know how it is?" I didn't, but I was about to find out.

"We resorted to crime, stealing bits and pieces from large stores in the beginning, living rough on the streets because we couldn't find work, and then getting hooked on weed and other substances. We were arrested a couple of times, not for anything serious of course, and we both spent time in jail, maybe a week or two, resolving that between us, we needed to get our act together, stay strong, and then try to find a job and a place to live. But the system just doesn't allow that. For some reason we became and we still are, entrenched in this no-win situation, obviously now we're here in San Francisco, where we cannot find work without and address and we cannot get an address without a job."

"Yes," I said, "It's all too familiar to me. I understand completely. But I am really curious as to why the city of Minneapolis gave you free tickets for a bus journey to San Francisco?"

Bob spoke.

"You see, the homeless up there are a nuisance to the city. They, the city council, project this cleaner than clean image for their town, and we, the homeless, just killed off that image by being out and visible on their precious streets. Some council member came up with this great plan, ship them out and rid the place of their nuisance, and, well, they did. They bought us all tickets to come to Cali. Some to LA and some to here. The promise of warm weather and a fresh start is too much to refuse for most"

"Wow!" I was blown away. What kind of world are we living in where a local authority decides that rather than fix their homeless issues, they should just dissolve that issue by sending them to another city to be someone else's problem? Pure madness. Rob and Bob definitely fit into my 'donation plans' and with that in mind, I quickly took out two of my $20 bills and passed them over to the guys.

"What's this?" asked Rob.

I told him I'd had a very lucrative day and that I wanted to share the spoils with two very nice genuine friends, but under no circumstances could they tell anyone that I'd been so generous.

"Why don't the 3 of us spend some time tomorrow and I'll see if I can pass on some tips to the two of you? Hopefully we will get lucky and you'll get a few more dollars in your pocket and maybe, just maybe, that will help you both get out of this mess?" I knew it wouldn't help, but I had to make my intentions positive and send an appealing message to both of them to motivate a response and hopefully to try and assist in making life a little more tolerable.

"Are you guys doing drugs, alcohol or anything else I should know about?" Rob shouted, "It's hard enough getting food without blowing money on that shit" "OK, keep the cash for emergencies for now and tomorrow we will see what else we can come up with." I got up, letting them know we would begin early the next day, and made my way to the other side of the room, sitting down next to an elderly couple, her, in tears, and him, trying unsuccessfully, to console her.

Orphaned and Homeless

Sitting alone against a cold brick wall
Birds, mainly scavengers, providing good company
Conversation limited to one-way dissertations
Laughing inwardly at his ability to charm
Adopted by chance through hunger
Remembering sadly that he had no other family

Years of walking to a place called nowhere
Abandoned by ignorance, educated by experience
Finding solace but only after numerous donations
Unable to come to terms with his lack of good fortune
Orphaned at twelve and homeless at sixteen
A citizen of a city inhospitable and dark

From day to day there seems no hope
Clinging to life through sheer determination
Prepared to die for a cause he did not create
Emptiness filling a confused and frightened mind
Never understanding why, he had become a statistic
Searching helplessly for a way out of hell

Offered bread and water and perhaps the occasional hot meal
Never receiving love that he so desires
Tears of his past becoming the strength of his future
Hardened and battle ready for the days that lie ahead
Knowing that life will be a lonely road that never ends
Accepting his plight with little respect for those who placed him there

"You doing OK?" I asked, my question directed to neither one of them in particular.

She, raised her saddened teary eyes, and just looked at me.

"Do I look like I am OK?" she said.

"You certainly do not. I am only trying to be nice" I replied, not knowing if that would kill the conversation stone dead, or encourage her to continue.

"I know" she continued, "but in here, no one is nice. I am so tired of all of this and I just want to die."

He piped up. "I found her this way about 30 minutes ago. She was slumped outside the shelter, crying her eyes out and really in a bad way."

"You did the right thing bringing her in here. They can look after her. I will get someone to talk to her" I told him.

She then took her tray of food and drew it closer to her body, as if to protect it from possible thievery.

"I am NOT talking to anyone" she insisted.

"Why?" I asked, "people in here are very nice and perhaps, just maybe, they can help you."

"I am beyond all help" she said.

"And why is that?" I asked.

The man then began to help her eat her meal by taking a spoon, handing it to her and encouraging her to take a bite.

"The food is good, I made some of it myself." I lied.

She was doubtful, and I could tell from her expression she didn't believe me.

"Where were you today?" I asked, as I tried to move the conversation along.

"Lying on a piece of grass near Union Square pondering my life and really curious as to why I have ended up here, homeless and destitute. I blamed God, then I blamed Jesus, and then I resigned myself to the fact that it's the fucking government that I need to resent, no one but the fucking government." Her response was filled with anger, but, the good thing was, she actually replied to me and our conversation was moving along in a positive manner.

He was about 75, and she must have been slightly younger, although it was really hard to tell. It's always difficult to guess accurately, the age of a homeless person. They are normally so beaten up by the elements, sleeping rough and suffering from the worst kinds of malnutrition, therefore guessing accurately is almost impossible. When I first saw them, I thought they were a couple, marching around the city together, looking to survive together, but now, after our brief but informative few words, I knew he'd just met her and she was really all alone out there, a realization that made me extremely sad.

How do women of this age, indeed how do woman of any age, survive on these streets? I'd had so many issues and been shit scared, so how must they feel and how do they keep themselves safe and sane? It's very difficult for a fit male to survive daily, and I could only image what this woman had been through.

"So," I asked her, "how'd you end up on the streets with the likes of me?" I smiled.

She relaxed. She began to eat. She began to talk. She began to make me feel like shit.

Ashamed

Looking around at the state of our cities
Feeling ashamed of the way we have evolved
Treating animals better that we treat the needy
Justifying policies to all people who voted
Politicians full of greed and self-importance
Running the country without care nor attention

Just look at these street people
Homeless and hungry with no roof to hide under
In the year 2022 we treat this as normality
Disgraceful behavior inside corridors of power
Leading to this anomaly that some call life
Living an existence most could not describe with words

Intelligence seems not our strongest facet
How much common sense would it take?
Leading these souls to a new Promised Land
Taking time out of party politics to make the difference
Saving them from further humiliation
Prioritizing dollars for human use and salvation

The truth shall be spoken one day
A real and true citizen of planet earth will speak out
The trash we have accumulated over centuries will be swept aside
Good people returning some life to those starved of it
Ceasing this outrageous frivolity and misuse
When once again the evolution process will start on an even keel

"My husband and I lived just south of Oakland. He had a great job, a truck driver, long distance. We were making great money, with his salary and mine combined, living well beneath our means and saving all the time. I was a school teacher. We'd had 1 child, a boy, who died when he was 12, drowned in a swimming pool, and so we soldiered on, doing the best we could, knowing I was too old to have more kids. Then, one day, my husband arrived home from a trip, feeling very unwell. We went to ER, and found out he was diabetic. No worries, they told us they would sort it out, regulate it and he'd be fine. The insurance covered most of what we had to spend on drugs and consultants, but then suddenly, about 18 months after being diagnosed, he got worse and had to give up his job and the insurance that came with it. My job was terminated for reasons I don't want to discuss, and that left the two of us, with a few dollars in the bank and facing huge medical bills as he deteriorated into a state which eventually required hospitalization. He was in there for about 6 weeks and unfortunately, they couldn't save him. Like I said, it's a very long story, and this is the short version. He passed away in January of last year, and that's when my life turned upside down. One minute I was in my home grieving and pondering my future alone and the next, after receiving bills from the hospital of over $300,000, bills which obviously I couldn't afford, I was forced to sell my home, pay the bills and I was left with nothing. Not one single penny. In fact, I still owe the hospital over $75,000. They'll never get that now, but anyway, after I sold my home, I moved in with a friend, who turned out to be a real bastard, and that left me with one option and one option only, walking these streets, alone, penniless and desperate. It's been over 7 months now and I have no idea how I've survived, nor do I know how long I can keep going. I had everything, and now I have absolutely nothing."

She was sobbing as she finished telling me her story, and I was too. How does one respond to a story like that? It's impossible and it's mind-boggling that this can happen to any human being. She's obviously not the only one in America who's had that happen to them, but for goodness' sake, don't you think someone somewhere should consider the cost of humanity above the cost of a few medical bills that can be written off in the interests of letting someone keep their home? I broke my hip in 2009, a biking accident, and ended up in hospital for 3 days. The bill was $86,465, I remember it to the exact penny, and all I had to pay for was the part my insurance company wouldn't cover, $245. I asked to see a copy of my bill and on the itemized list of all the things I'd been given while there, were cost for gloves, several box full of gloves, more gloves than I could have used in a lifetime, and for drugs I hadn't taken and many other items that seemed odd, like pillowcases and sheets. Anyway, I called the billing department and asked them to clarify this list and asked also why it was $86 grand for three days when most of this list was made up or fake. Her exact words to me, and I will never forget this,

"Mr. Zoltie, we have a deal with your insurance company, you only pay the $245 and they will take care of the rest. Your real total is about $36,000, and the balance, which is more than half of your total, and which they pay for too, will go into a fund for patients that have no coverage."

WTF???

Patients that have no coverage are being taken care of by an excess to a bill I have received, an excess which is manufactured to encourage fraud and then care for people who have no insurance? What kind of system is that? And then, and then you talk to someone like this woman in the shelter and you have to question where this 'system' was when she needed it most. This whole country is a fucked-up mess, and that story she told me and the hospital visit I had is direct proof that 'fucked-up mess' might not be language that's strong enough to describe what goes on in the United States of America, where nothing at all is United, other than the money we all spend. I take issue not only with this lady's story, but the manner in which she found herself exiled to homeless status, without any chance of reprieve of adjudication by those in authority. And, by the way, she is not and was not alone with stories that played out in similar fashion, stories I have heard in person, over many years of working with homeless people. In this day and age, with homelessness overwhelming all of our cities, climbing to unprecedented levels and every single governor, senator and local legislator, along with celebrities, volunteers and so many others, preaching for an end to this pandemic, why oh why does anyone end up on the streets because of an unpaid medical bill? As I said before, it's inhumane, so obviously insane and lacking in any common sense that a solution, a simple solution, cannot be found. Prevention could be half the cure, but more of that to come later in this book.

I held her hand and the old guy she was with got off his chair and put his arm around her trying to make her feel safe and wanted. And the he said,

"Something similar happened to me, only I have kids who discarded me as a piece of shit, knowing I would be walking these streets while they live in nice homes, drive fabulous cars and enjoy all the benefits of the great jobs that keep them infused with all these luxuries."

"What do you mean?" I asked.

"Well, how long do you have?"

"I'm going nowhere, and I don't think she is either?" I said as I pointed to the old lady.

And so, he began.

"I'd just turned 52, and was enjoying much success as a carpenter, a profession I'd pursued since I was a teenager. I was always good with my hands. I could make things from wood that other people only dreamed about, and I was a true craftsman, an artisan, one might say. I started my own business when I was 35, I'd been married about 7 years, we'd had two kids, one boy and one girl, who both were given everything in life that any kid could ask for. We spoiled them rotten, and as my business grew and my workload increased, I spent more time in my office than I did at home, breeding a resentment with my wife and kids that festered and then grew into a battle that became a torrid divorce, that eventually led to my losing not only my family, but my business, my home and my sanity and then ending up here, on these streets, with nothing. Absolutely nothing! That was 20 years ago, and I have not seen any of them since the divorce was finalized, and my wife, who ran off with my closest friend, turning both kids against me in a manner that's inconceivable, doesn't care on iota that I have ended up here, destitute. In fact, no one cared that I lost everything, including my sanity, no one cared I ended up with a drink issue that teetered on the brink of alcoholic poisoning, and no one, not one of them, batted an eyelid when I ended up on these streets, which by the way, they knew about, and never offered to help or tried to remedy. They're all a bunch of ungrateful people, that I treated with respect and looked after each and every one of them, only to end up like this, with nothing, no family, no friends and also no hope."

I was stunned. How could any family member allow their father to live on the streets while they enjoyed their comforts of home and all the luxuries life has to give? It just made no sense.

"Do you ever try to contact your kids?" I asked, "Can I call them for you?" "Ha!" he replied, "the last time I called my son, who lives about ten blocks from here and works for some tech company, making over 6 figures a year, he told me to 'go fuck myself' and then put the phone down. So, I went to where he lives and stood outside until one day, I actually saw him leaving his building with a lovely lady by his side. I made an approach, but before I got within 10 yards of him, he recognized me, pulled the young lady closer to his side, and jumped into a waiting cab, flipping me the finger as the cab drove off. I didn't give up, and I hung around that building for a few more days in the hope he'd feel guilty and at least try to offer up some form of contact. He knew where I was, and he looked at me each time he left, and then again when he returned from work.

Nothing! Blanked me as if I didn't exist, which in his mind, I don't. There I was, standing like a moron, not moving, staring at his building, day after day, when one morning, around 10AM, I got a tap on my shoulder. This suit, a tall guy, dressed nicely, asked me if I was Josh Hart, and I nodded. He then thrust a paper into my hand and told me that he's served me with a restraining order and that if I came withing 200 yards of this building, the one where my son lived, I would be arrested and jailed. I looked at him straight in the face and said, "do you think I care? Jail would be much better than these streets, and at least I'd have people to talk to. He didn't give a hoot, and instead of listening to what I had to say, he walked off. I walked after him, eventually ending up by his side, and telling him in no uncertain terms where he could stick his papers, as I ripped them up in front of his face. I continued to stand in front of my son's building for another 3 days, not eating, only drinking water, knowing he was watching me, even though I couldn't see him. He must have used a back entrance or some other devious method of avoidance, because I have never seen him since. Don't even know if he's still in the same apartment building. I just gave up."

My initial thoughts were to ask him where that building was and go round there myself and try to find his son and talk some sense into him, but instead I asked,

"And your daughter, where's she?"

"No idea" he replied as put his head in his hands and began to sob.

No Water

They took it away
Emptied
Gone, but where to?
Life, placed on hold
Quiet, ever so quiet
No water, therefore no hope of continuation

They sit, staring at this empty hole
Pondering
Thoughts wrapped up in silence
Asking that very same question
Together in one voice
How will we survive?

The two of them had made such an impression on me that I decided to blow all I had in the way of cash and split it between them. I also suggested that they join me the following day and that we spending time together, along with Rob and Bob, perhaps trying hard to come to terms in my own mind that if I was given time, I might have an opportunity to delve deeper into all of their psyche's and hopefully turn things around for all of them, no matter how small that turn would be. It seemed hilarious to me that on day one I'd met Oleg, and joined his gang and here I was, on the brink of my last full day in the city and I was going to have my own following, or gang. How ironic, how utterly depressing but also, how uplifting. To find someone who was willing to put their trust in you, especially a homeless person, knowing their trust levels were bordering on the non-existent, was an honor indeed.

I handed over every penny I had to the two of them, leaving me enough money for train fare home, which was greeted with more than just appreciation. They both sat there speechless and we all hugged one more time.

"I know it's not much" I said, "but tomorrow, all of us can try hard to make more, and I am certain we will succeed"

I knew the chances were slim, but making money on my last day wasn't going to be a priority. At least not for me. I was determined to find a solution for my four new friends and at least attempt to get them off the streets, even if it was temporary, for the good of their health, and their minds. The older two were obviously a priority and I made a note to chat to Stevie first thing in the morning, hopefully to get them some kind of work in his shelter. A long shot perhaps, but a shot I was willing to take.

When night arrived and I was all 'tucked' up on my bunk, I heard a really strange noise coming from nearby. Now, realizing that there are many strange people bunked up together, snoring and shouting out loud while sleeping being a common practice amongst most of them, it's not hard to imagine who might be trying to sleep with who. Yes, it does go on. These people are just like you and I when it comes to their sexual needs and desires and although some of them might be a little perverted, smelly, uncouth or just plain horny, and although men outnumber the women by more than 4 to 1, sex is very common practice at night and those who decide to partake, leave very little to the imagination and are not in the least embarrassed by their carnal desires being heard, seen or yes, smelt!

Anyway, this noise stated to get louder and louder and it occurred to me that whoever was in mid-flow fucking, wasn't just fucking one, buy maybe several women at the one time. The thing is, at nighttime in the shelter, although you want to relax and shut down to sleep, it's almost impossible, well at least it was for me. With one eye on who's trying to steal from you, another on who might assault you and one more, yes, that 3rd eye, looking out for anyone who encroaches on your space, sleep rarely, if ever is satisfying or comfortable. Noise is the largest issue, followed by disgusting odors and then fear. I think the most continuous, uninterrupted sleep I got on any of my six nights was about 1.5 hours at a time. When I returned home, I slept almost 24 hours straight, but we will come to that.

This feeling I had that this noise was a kind of orgy taking place was becoming stronger and stronger, and I decided to open one eye and maybe look around quickly without arousing suspicion that I was peeping. I turned onto my left side, I opened one eye and then the other, waiting for them to adjust to the semi darkness, and there, there it was. This guy, this horrible ugly man, was humping someone, or was it something? I couldn't quite tell but the noise was decidedly annoying and loud and more and more of the shelter's population were waking from their slumber to the same tune, some of them furious, some just curious. I sat up, and I looked over towards the fracas coming from this man's bed. I focused, not quickly, but eventually, just enough to check and confirm that what I was looking at wasn't a mistake and that I was witnessing exactly what I thought I was looking at. It was true! He was having sex with this semi-inflated, inflatable sex doll! The doll was squeaking, the man was humping and between them the noise was that of an orgy. Hump, squeak, hump hump, squeak. It went on and on, and he was talking to the doll as if it was a real woman. "Come on bitch, fuck me, feel my balls, ride that cock" he would say. It was like something out of One Flew Over the Cuckoo's Nest. The guy had obviously retrieved this doll out of a trash can, because it was filthy and, probably smelly, fancying his chances of getting laid while everyone slept. He was making a good go of it too, but then someone who was lying closer than I was, became so fed up with the shenanigans going down, that he walked up to the bunk, ripped the doll away from under the guy who was fucking it and, with a fork he'd obviously stolen or kept from dinner service, proceeded to stab the doll to death, a horrible death, while the guy who'd been fucking it, lay prostate on his bunk, looking like someone just stole his favorite toy and he couldn't do anything about it. Which, by the way, was actually true! He looked lost and the man who'd stabbed the doll to its final death, looked triumphant. Well, I wasn't getting involved, but I could tell that all hell was about to break loose, so I retreated back to my bunk and lay down and waited for the fun to start.

It didn't take long.

The doll murderer also sensed trouble and with that in mind, he pointed his fork towards the guy who had been fucking the doll but was now doll-less, and told him that if he tried anything, he'd be next to be deflated. I found this hilarious because his fork was very small and probably blunt. The night staff and some of the other residents were now alerted and a posse was being formed as battle lines were being drawn. The man with the fork knew this of course, and as quickly as he'd been a murderer, he was back lying down on his bunk displaying a look that resembled nothing but the innocence of a child. The other guy, the victim, (although it's fair to say the real victim had been the doll), went for the guy with the fork. As he lunged towards this man's bunk, what he didn't see or know was that right behind him, the night staff had gathered, all prepared to get involved and to break up this melee before it had even begun. They grabbed him, the doll-less man, by the back of his head, holding his hair as they did so. His head flung back in a position that looked painful enough to break his neck. He yelled, which disturbed the equilibrium that nighttime brings to a shelter. Everyone was up. I sensed a riot brewing, and it was boiling faster than any kettle I've even known could boil. A rapid descent of all decency ensued. The 'inmates', having been alerted to the possibility of an all-out brawl, went into protective mode or survival mode, depending on their physical condition or willingness to get involved in a fight. That meant more than half of those who were asleep were now gathering their belongings and hiding themselves and their gear, under their blankets. The other half, the fighters, we up and about, shouting, goading, screaming, at all of the staff members who just wanted this all to go away or to take place on someone else's watch. Too late. A brawl commenced, punches thrown, kicks attempted by feet that were mostly shoeless and everyone involved was barking out expletives by the dozen in this battle to end all battles. It lasted about two minutes, when, without warning, all the interior lights came on and the heavy mob, the staff who'd been in a different room, hurtled into the dorm and tried to stamp out the row as quickly as possible. The guy who'd deflated the doll rolled under the sheet on his bunk, protesting his innocence and the victim of the crime, the doll, was brought out from under his bunk as evidence that he was definitely full of shit. The man who'd lost the doll to the murderer, wouldn't sit down or go back to sleep, insisting he'd been robbed and relieved of his prize possession before he could indeed relieve himself. The moral of the story being? Don't be a pussy with a fake pussy. Get yourself a real one. That's what the guards told him as they helped him pack his bags up and escorted him into another room to spend the remainder of his night while the rest of us got back to sleep. It was 11.30 PM, and no one was happy, no one was rested, and no one was going to sleep at all that night.

Walked Away

He got up and he just walked away
Roaming unchallenged into a crowded street
Carrying nothing other than the burden he had become accustomed to
Seen dripping from his weary shoulders to his bare feet
Dark and stained from relentless pounding
Discolored by miles and miles of a journey to nowhere

Head buried deep in sadness
Hanging from shoulders that were once so broad
Facing downwards towards each painful footstep
Wondering why life had not ended on this corner of hate
Keeping him alive for a reason he would never fathom
Certainly not to carry out the work of the Lord, his once esteemed God

He had been no Moses, no Abraham and no use to anyone
So he thought
His life, a parable of one he'd read about with love
Trying to emulate his hero, his savior
Passing the will of the past to those with a very bleak future
Succumbing unnecessarily into the arms of the devil himself

A do-gooder, they'd mocked him as a pariah
Turning inside out his case for recognition
Twisting his somewhat simple mind into unfashionable common sense
Ignoring, willingly, his right to help their existence
Defeating, purposely, an attempt to be their champion
Sending a clear-cut message to a man who believed he could make a
difference

Now, as one of them, he had lost all sense of being
Condemned for life to saving his own soul
Looking out desperately for an opportunity to relieve his pain
Not brave enough to command an early self-inflicted exit
Unwilling and unable, he would serve his days as persona non grata
Walking away in a straight line that would end only when his mind became untwisted

Treat them like human beings and perhaps they will feel like human beings? Treat them like dogs and they will behave like animals. That's not a quote from anyone in particular, it's just the way I feel about our homeless problem, not only here in America, but all over the world. Of course, if they want to live like animals, and don't get me wrong, some of them really do like being on the streets, then there's nothing we can do to change that mentality. It's a given that some people just like that way of life and we, as a society, pander to their desires by opting to promote that lifestyle through government programs which supply these people with everything they want. I just read an interview and watched a video recording made by a homeless guy in San Francisco. As I write this page, it's February 10 2022. In the interview, the man concerned was brutal in his contempt for society and goading in his gratitude to our government for supplying him with $650 a month in the way of a stipend, enabling him not to go looking for work. This money pays for his Netflix and Amazon Prime subscriptions, he also gets, courtesy of Sprint/T-Mobile, a cell phone with unlimited calling and data, and the remainder of this windfall he spends on drugs to fuel his abuse. All of his food and board he gets for free already, just by going to a shelter at night. What an existence! And who is paying? WE are!!

It's all backwards. There are real homeless people out there who get so little, and there are of course, system abusers, like this man. With tattoo's all over his face, (yes, who paid for them?), and the rest of his body, and with his brand-new iPhone 13 strapped to his waist, and his Amazon Prime membership, again, paid for by another government program that you and I are funding, what purpose does this guy have in his life other than to remain a taker and abuser of government programs that you and I, the tax payer, fund? Our society is crumbling under the effects that homelessness has on everyday life. Look at Venice Beach and Santa Monica. Both used to be great tourist spots, have amazing beaches and parks and some of the best restaurants. Now, with over 45,000 homeless people encamped in drug infested, insanitary, tented cities, all which, have sprung up since 2018. These cities, along with so many other cities across this country, have been devastated by a pandemic of such relevance, that our local governments have missed their opportunities to stop it from spreading and as out of control as it seems to be right now, in 2 to 3 more years from now, if nothing changes, and it's highly unlikely it will, things will be so bad, it'll drive these towns back into the dark ages, from which their chances of recovery will be zero. The question is, how to do we stop this issue from getting any worse, or indeed, can we actually stop it from spreading into uncontrollable regress? The answer is very simple, probably not, at least not with the way the Federal and local governments think at this precise moment in time. Many people have put their minds into trying to resolve this problem, and most of them have more intelligence than I do, but to date, even with the tens of millions of dollars that have been thrown at trying to cure this issue, the problem has only gotten worse, and there's no sign of any improvement whatsoever. It's all well and good giving money, food, tiny homes, shelters, free phones, drug friendly areas and all the other BS that we have tied doing to fix our, not so little, problem, but none of the above seems to work, in fact I think it's fair to say that going by the situation we currently find ourselves in, everything has indeed, failed! The question is, what would work? Well, having accumulated so many years of experience with homelessnes, some of which you have read in this book, I have formulated a plan, not a simple plan, a rather complicated plan, but a plan nonetheless. It's a plan that would take several years to implement, be dependent on all parts of government, local and federal, working in unison, without any partisan bias, and a plan that could change the landscape of our cities and return all of our lives, both homeless and normal lives, back into the lives we all hoped for and deserve. No one, I repeat, no one, not a single human being, deserves to be homeless, and it's the purpose of all of us to try to make that situation evaporate into something that becomes a thing of our pasts, and never to be experienced again in our futures. Almost an impossibility, but let's see, perhaps it's not just the pipe dream you might think it to be.

What Finally Made Me Snap

Many times before and probably many times more
Walking through this cesspit called society
Looking in both directions, one, very carefully
Searching out glory in an inglorious situation
Amongst the poor and the rich, amongst confusion
And then, what finally made me snap

Children, adults and those who claim to be human
Urinating, defecating, masturbating
A collective audience that should be hidden
Visible for many reasons, all-wrong
The dregs of a theatre called depravity
Opening its curtains for the world to stare

Passing by again and again, eyes shielded by disgust
Appreciating each and every painful moment
Wondering why, and wondering out loud
Seething, as each case becomes monotonous and repetitious
Stacked against a backdrop that could be beautiful
Instead, a scorching sun, lighting up pure ugliness

Heavens that seemed to have vanished, flush with promise
Sky blue as they offer respite to those who pray
False impressions found inside loneliness
Hunger, the food in which all of the unfortunate digest
Begging aimlessly for scraps and coins that fall so infrequently
Manna, though not biblical, certainly relevant

How and why, two questions that will remain forever unanswered
Permanent reminders that nothing can be perfect
A battle, ongoing through eternity, fought by lost souls
Won in the end by the grace of God
Putting a stop to this struggle that should never have been
Justified by a reluctance to find an everlasting solution

My Plan

We have millions of acres of empty land, here in the USA, most of it protected or located in areas that, to date, have been declared as uninhabitable or just not close enough to the cities where people like to live. These plots of empty land exist in almost every single state that makes up the Union. What we forget is that in the past, these places were inhabited by an indigenous population or by people who just wanted to get away from the hustle and bustle of what we all call, every-day life. These land masses, are vast, they are empty and they *are* inhabitable, especially with today's technology, if we wanted them to be. Let's take San Jose California as just one example. San Jose lies 50 miles south of San Francisco. It's the heart of Silicon Valley, and in the last 40 years, the population of that city has increased from 180,000 to over 1 million, all of whom live in approximately the same landmass as its original inhabitants enjoyed all these years ago, but perhaps in a more condensed manner. The difference? We have destroyed green space, orchards, hills and the likes, just to accommodate an influx, and we've built homes, office space and many manufacturing plants. The original settlers of the city of San Jose would never recognize the place if they came back to see it in 2022. Of course, that's progress and progress for the better, so we are told. Now, if you go 30 miles south and east of San Jose, towards a town called Gilroy, there lies a body of land, just between Gilroy and Los Banos, which is a small town that sits on the I-5 interstate, the freeway that runs from Seattle to San Diego. That huge acreage of land, which encompasses tens of thousands, if not millions of acres of empty space, I'm sure is habitable. Now, don't get me wrong here, I've picked a piece of land in an area I know. I am no geologist or environmental scientist; nor do I claim to have any inclination if what I am about to propose is even feasible, but when you have the basis of a plan, that plan has to start somewhere. This piece of land could really be any piece of land in America, I am sure there are thousands of pieces just like it, empty, just like other land/space which is now occupied, was 100 years ago, such as San Jose. Land that's situated near cities, but land that's unused and land that has the possibility to be exploited for the purpose of habitation, and one day, as our population increases, probably will be.

Giving money to any homeless person is not only kind, and heartwarming from the giver's standpoint, but it's often irresponsible. Anybody giving, never quite knows if that money will go to help buy food, drink or drugs, or all of the above. It's often more sensible to offer to buy a homeless person a meal, or to take them home and bathe and feed them, although the chances of anyone offering that kind of charity to a homeless person in this day and age, is slim to zero.

Giving money creates an endless cycle of, cash = drugs = alcohol, and sometimes food. I have seen it, lived it and watched it repeat itself a million times over. I realize that some of you reading this will have a completely different opinion, but trust me here, and hear me out, throwing money the way we all throw money at this problem is only fueling the issue to the extent that it cannot get better. If everyone who was homeless used the cash they were given in a responsible manner then there would be no issue. The fact is, they don't. Some do, most don't. It's a fact.

So, what can we do? Instead of donating money to individuals we randomly meet and feel sorry for, we stop doing it altogether. We implore local authorities to start land planning and we dedicate land, even if it's waste land, to build a city/town/village only for homeless people. We do this not by regular means, using licensed contractors/labor, (although we would definitely need their support and assistance), but we let the homeless do it themselves with the help of donations of materials instead of money, giving them all the opportunity to build not only their own homes, but the opportunity to regain their self-esteem. This is what most of them are missing, a purpose in life, a means to an end, an address to get a job, a job to get an address. We implore large corporations to donate materials and not cash. We implore volunteers/trade professionals to donate time, and not cash. We implore builders to donate their expertise and not cash. We help build homes for those who do not have any! A city for the homeless, built by the homeless and then lived in by homeless people who then have a distinct purpose in life to succeed. Naïve?? Perhaps, but let me ask you this. If you were a homeless person, and again, I know all homeless people don't want the same thing, but wouldn't you give your right arm to help build a home that one day would be your own? Not only homes, but shops and services too, such as doctors' offices, clinics, health care programs, all of this would be possible, with the right management and the support of all of us who want to see an end to this disease, this pandemic, this injustice. With professional help, government assistance, (let's face it, the billions that are wasted at that level every year is mind-blowing), a little bit of compassion and a lot of faith, this might just be the solution that every local authority in America needs. It's not really a figment of my imagination, it's just a good old sensible idea, one which you may shoot down in flames in a heartbeat, but try and come up with a better plan? If you can, I am here to listen. Are all the 2.5 million homeless people in America going to be able to live on our streets forever? Perhaps they can, but more probably, they cannot. Remember, the average age of a homeless person in the USA is 9! That's a cardinal sin right there, allowing children to be homeless in a society that is rich beyond words.

We are gifted with the technology, we have the brain power, we know how much we waste on a daily basis, not only food, but clothing, wood, nuts, bolts, and the list goes on. Let's stop the waste and put it to good use. If you were homeless, and think about this for a minute or two, wouldn't you want to live with a roof over your head? Wouldn't you want to retain your self-esteem and enjoy a place in normal society? Of course, you would, and the incredible fact is, we have so much land in America, how difficult would it be to experiment with this idea and implement a test program to see if I am right or not? We, as residents of the cities and towns we live in, do not want homeless people roaming our streets, making us feel uncomfortable, making us wish we could just sweep them aside or put them on busses which will take them to other cities, just to clean up our mess. No, we would be delighted to help make them comfortable inside their own homes, with jobs to go to and contributions to society to look forward to as well. You and I are paying for this problem, so why can't we try to pay for the cure? Our country is wealthy beyond belief, so let's use that wealth and distribute it in a way that might fix this issue. The land mass I'm suggesting, no matter where it is, will eventually be built on, and we can give all of these unfortunates a head start by assisting in that development and bringing a brighter future to all of them, especially the kids. At the end of the day, there will always be those who choose to be homeless, but the vast majority do not desire that way of life, nor did they ask for it in the first place.

Ode to a Rat

Mr. Rat, you run so fast
Darting through the smallest of spaces
Surprising me as your tail brushed my leg
They laughed out loud
How silly
Terrified, they should have run
Like you, they want to eat and sleep
No attempt to destroy your life
Giggling uncontrollably, probably with fear

Mr. Rat you climb so high
Escaping the clutches of those who hate you
Hastily retreating to some place dark
You have found your path
One after another twelve rungs are scaled
Hiding now inside this roof
Feeding heartily with your friends
Perhaps sharing your catch with family
No longer visible, erasing their fear

Mr. Rat, we shall never meet again
Breakfast is cooked but remains uneaten
Your presence diminished my already small appetite
Knowing from which direction you came
Unable to comprehend your possible nuisance
My life is worthy of missing one meal
Safety I shall find in complete abstinence
Never to return to this table or room
Your body quite small your impact so large.

My last day! Or should I say, my last full day. I still had the full day, that particular night and then part of the following day to get through.

None of us had slept well after the commotion we'd witnessed first-hand that previous evening. The culprit, who's inflatable doll was now discarded in the trash, was made to sleep on the floor in another room, alone and in disgrace, and now, as the sun rose up to welcome yet another day on these vile streets, he was being lectured by one of the shelter's staff and told in no uncertain terms that any repeat of last night's antics would mean no more shelter, no more food and no more of anything other than rejection from this place that he called, his home. Harsh treatment indeed, although fully warranted.

I gathered my new 'gang' together for a pep talk. Funny how things turn around. There I was, a leader of sorts, with 4 other hapless human beings, all with potential, hidden somewhere within, all now ready to follow like sheep, just in case we struck gold. Breakfast was a sweet bun and bottled water, and then we were all kicked out and into what had now become the most regular of routines for all of them, other than me. There was Rob and Bob, the old man and lady, who eventually I would call Fred and Ginger, after the famous dance due of the 1940's and 50's, and we were ready, willing, but hardly able. The two younger guys were a real pain in the ass. Rob and Bob were typical millennials, although at that time, millennials didn't exist. I swear, even to this day, that these kids were the epitome of what was to come. They moaned about everything, complaining all the time about the way they were treated, the lack of respect they received, the money they deserved, and really, by the time we'd packed up and were ready to leave the shelter, which was around 7.30 AM, I'd already had my fill of both of them. Taking a deep breath, I decided enough was enough and pulling both to one side, I delivered my 'Zoltie' lecture.

"Guys," I began, "I'm done with your moaning, your bitching and complaining. I've had it with the way you feel about everything. Remember guys, no one put you here, you chose to be here. I know your lives have been difficult, but so has everyone else's lives in that shelter and some have faced a lot more difficulties than you. You guys need to realize that you're only 20 years of age. Look at Fred and Ginger over there. They're in their 60's and 70's and what hope do they have? You have youth on your side, so perhaps, and I know it's not easy, you need to take a long look in the mirror and figure out why and how you got here and what and when you can change this situation to make your lives a little more comfortable. It'll do no good for any of us, especially Fred and Ginger, if you bitch about everything and you carry on doing it all day long. If you do want to go in that direction, feel free, but do it on your own. I don't need you and neither do they" I said, as I pointed to Fred, who was now sitting down on a bench, looking like he wasn't going to budge. He was exhausted, he looked completely beaten by this curse of being homeless, and he looked ready to die. I felt terrible, he was obviously hurting, and there I was, dishing out advise to two frightened, miserable, unfortunates, who, through no fault of their own, were stuck in this homeless bubble that never looked like it would burst and they had no idea who to talk to or who to ask for help in order that their lives might change, even just a little, for the better. It was time for a change of tact. I had verbally attacked them and now it was time to be a little more compassionate.

I continued,

"Guys, look. Here's the deal. The world hates you as much as it hates me and it hates everyone who doesn't have a regular life with a home, an income, a job and a family. Nobody asked to be homeless, let alone wants to be homeless, so the question is, what are you guys going to do to end this misery and to get back into society with jobs and a place to stay? Do you really want to get out of the shit you're in?" Rob spoke first.

"What do you think? At first this was fun, but neither of us thought it would last. We were on an adventure, and that adventure turned into a road trip and we both believed the road trip with end with a pot of gold that we'd split and live happily ever after. But look at us now? We're abandoned by our families, the system, and every other human being who walks on the earth. We are seen as parasites, beggars of the worst type and how can we possibly get out of something that seems never-ending?" He was right. They'd been abandoned even by God and there really was no place to go. I began to wonder why I'd even bothered to offer them hope that day? It seemed so futile that here I was, rich in so many ways, faking my existence as a homeless man and unable to tell them the truth, yet very able to give them money and advice that might one day help them get out of their mess. The issue was, if I helped them, did I help Fred and Ginger too? And if I helped Fred and Ginger, who should I help next and when does it all stop? Then you realize that you cannot possibly help everyone? And that is exactly what motivated me to complete this book. The only possible way to help them all was to advocate for better resources, more money, more of everything, to make it plausible for some of our homeless community to get new lives, new hope, a roof over their heads and most importantly, their self-esteem back.

After this little chat, it was time to set off in search of some cash, a bite to eat and perhaps some other good fortune, which maybe, just maybe, we could all conjure up. In my opinion, before we'd taken one single step, I realized, with a rude awakening, that this was going to be one of the most difficult days I had ever had in my entire life. I hadn't bargained for a posse, but now I had one. Each one with a different issue and each one, placing hope in my positivity and encouragement. Unbeknown to them, of course, was the fact that really, I wasn't one of them. I was a fraud, but a fraud giving them an opportunity to start to believe in themselves and maybe, just maybe, one day they would be in a better place than any of them had begun that day.

Lying Asleep Surrounded by Life

On a magic carpet he lays
Oblivious to life as it passes casually by
Emptiness, filling a head with no direction
Death, closer than he will ever believe
Sleeping off the effects of yesterday
Waking soon to his troubles of today

Purple haze, like a halo, surrounding his weary head
Passersby, stepping lightly over this embarrassment
Interest peaking as that unfamiliar odor illuminates fresh air
Looking down with resentment at this unwanted gift
Paralyzed temporarily by their fear
Determined to ignore, destined to feel sad

A penny or two on top of his well-worn coat
Thrown there by those who feel their need to give, though not generously
Gently landing on the numbness of mockery
Unused during this period of comatose thankfulness
Left for another day, perhaps a happier one
Found someplace other than the grass where life now deteriorates rapidly

When I walk, I walk at quite a fast pace. I can comfortably stride at 4 miles per hour, something I have always been capable of. I used to run a lot too. My legs are strong, and I get three meals a day and can drink water whenever I like. Most of you reading this book will be in a similar position, and most of you will never know what it's like not to be able to do what you want, when you want and indeed as often as you want. Most of you are strong, willing and able.

Fred and Ginger however, well, that was a problem. They couldn't walk, didn't want to walk and when, with a little encouragement, they did walk, it was so painfully slow, so alien to my way of moving, that it almost drove me to a point of telling them I had to leave then to their own devices because mentally I just couldn't cope. I have a very A type personality, and on that day, I needed to climb down from my pedestal, realizing that they were more important than I was, and adjust my expectations to accommodate them and not me. It wasn't easy to do, in fact, it took every ounce of patience I had, and I don't have very much, to make them feel that they were part of this 'group' we'd formed. Rob and Bob weren't as bad as me in the sense that they were used to bumming around begging for cash and didn't move that fast, but honestly they were in their teens so they had the ability to keep up if necessary. From the get-go I wondered if I'd made a mistake offering council and company to all 4? In the end, I had to put all thoughts of abandoning Fred and Ginger out of my head in the hope that I could make some kind of difference in their lives that day, no matter how small that difference might be. I didn't really know why I wanted to make a difference, I just did. I followed my gut feeling and we started our 'march' towards sustenance and possible financial reward. Our initial idea was to walk back up Market St to the tram station and then, provided Fred and Ginger were still willing and able, to make a B-line for the San Francisco Giants baseball stadium, where an afternoon game would take place. I knew that ballpark sold out every week and the guarantee of over 40,000 people with money, was just too good to pass up. Someone attending that game would donate to our cause, I was sure of it, the only problem that I saw was how we were going to portray our gang? Would we all beg together, individually, in twos? I just didn't know and I had to figure it out quickly. I knew I personally could do almost anything to make people part with their cash, but the rest of them? Rob and Bob were too young and a little too aggressive and Fred and Ginger, too old and not aggressive enough. What a combination to be 'lumbered' with. We were almost at the tram stop when I pulled everyone to one side and unveiled my strategy.

"Listen up. We need to make a concerted effort to be nice to everyone we meet today. I'm not saying that you're nasty, but Rob, Bob, you guys especially, if you want to get cash to survive, being nice is a plus, and aggressiveness is a definite no go"

I looked at both Rob and Bob, and I could see confusion written all over their faces.

I continued

"Look, I know you're two good guys, so don't take this to heart. I just know that being extra nice will bring its benefits. I would also ask you to 'smarten' yourselves up, but I know that's impossible, so, at the end of the day the way you talk to people and the less aggressive you are towards them, the more successful you can be. Watch me."

I crossed over to the opposite side of the road and approached a couple who seemed to be debating whether to get in line for the tram or not. I decided to take matters into my own hands and make their decision for them.

"You know, if you are very clever you can walk about half a mile to the next stop and get on without waiting in line?" I told them. They were surprised at first, looking me up and down with some disdain, but after my suggestion sunk in, which only took a second or two, the man, who seemed quite affable, took my suggestion with the intent it was meant and asked me where they had to get to if they wanted to jump on at the next stop.

"If you give me a few bucks, I will take you" I said, believing at the same time they would just tell me to get lost.

"Just point us in the right direction, and we will find it" he told me, and as he said this, his right hand went into his right jacket pocket and at that point, I knew I was going to be rewarded for my audacity.

He pulled out a bill of unknown denomination, and after putting firmly into my left hand, thanked me and walked off with his wife in the direction of the tram stop I'd told them about. I crossed back over the road and explained to my posse what I'd done and then looked at the money he'd given me for the first time.

It was $5, not too shabby for a few seconds of brilliance! The others, I hoped, could now see how easy it had been. Their eyes had been opened and it hadn't taken me more than a minute to make them realize what their potential could be.

"Listen, all the other people out here begging for money are doing just that, begging. We need to be different; we need to be cunning and we need to be clear to anyone we approach that we are nice people, a little unfortunate, but nice. Got it?"

They all nodded in the affirmative.

"Ok, here's what we do. Fred and Ginger will go over there," and I pointed to the corner of Market and Leavenworth. "Rob and Bob, go up Market for two blocks and stand on the corner of Polk. Look for tourists, only tourists. If you're not sure who is and who isn't a tourist, then pass and move on to your next possible victim. Be certain they aren't locals. Locals don't donate to people like us. Tourists can be determined by their accents, maps that they carry, bored kids being dragged around behind them, and clothes that they wear, clothes we wouldn't consider American." I knew what I meant by this last statement, but I wasn't sure they did. "When you find a tourist, be helpful, be nice, offer assistance, suggestions on where to go, to eat, to play, and do it with determination and with an air of grace." Everyone nodded again, but I was skeptical. I had no idea what was going to happen, nor did I have any control, but I had indeed given them inspiration and I could see by their eyes that they were fired up and raring to go.

"Look, it's almost 9 AM, lets meet back here around 10.30, and whatever you make you keep, except for me. Whatever I make, I will give to the person who's made the most out of the 4 of you" More inspiration, and now, they were in a competition, a competition they all wanted to win.

"So," said Rob, "you're not keeping anything you make today?"
"No, it's all or nothing with you guys. You have the day with me, and tomorrow who knows where I will be" I said, knowing full well I would be on my way home to my own bed and my old life. "So go out, enjoy what you are doing, put a smile of hope on your hapless faces and let's try to make some cash."

It had been a rallying call, and one that looked like it might work. Time would tell.

We all split up, Ginger and Fred walking slowly towards their chosen corner and Rob and Bob sprinting towards theirs, shouting repeatedly at one another as they ran, "I'll win", "NO I will!"

No matter what was going to happen, no matter how much or how little they would make, no matter how easy or how hard it would be, I had managed to instill a little inspiration and hope into some very sad frightened people and I had given them an opportunity to gain some of their self-esteem back, just by treating them like the human beings they deserved to be. Calling them all by their first names. Making sure they had someone who could guide them, and all the time, listening to their concerns and adding some kind of advice into their daily routine, which, by now, had become laborious and disorderly. They had, for the first time in a long time, structure in yet, another awful day, living rough on the streets of San Francisco. The obvious question was, how would they cope, if at all?

Jaw Breaker

At a bar, in the middle of nowhere, he sits
Baseball cap covering his slim face
Looking nowhere other than downwards
Feeding station for his hunger
A bowl, filled with repetitive indigestion
Gulped down, piece by piece
A non-stop experience for the record books

One going down, whilst another is still in his mouth
No breaks, a complete eating machine
Jawbreaker on speed
His drug of selection, covered in red sauce
Mission of completion, his priority
Soaking up none of this dull atmosphere
Just filling his never-ending thirst for food

Was their wellbeing, (my new gang), and ability to cope with their situation, really my problem? Why them and not any of the other 30 or 40,000 homeless people in that city? I didn't know and I had no time to worry about it. I wanted to try to get as much cash on this final day as I possibly could and then split it all amongst them, and even though I'd told them winner takes all, I had no intention of letting any of them leave without getting something. With the four of them now positioned at different points along Market St, my plan was to disappear into another part of the Tenderloin district or to shoot up to Chinatown and spend an hour there, just to see if I could persuade some of the locals to give me anything in the way of cash or food. The problem with the locals is that they're so sick and tired of living with this homeless problem on their doorstep, homeless people are no longer human beings to them, they are classed as pests. I couldn't blame them for having that attitude, after all, living with so many vagrants day in and day out must be tiresome and off-putting, especially for those who run businesses and have homeless people camping day and night right on their doorsteps. And I use that word, camping, literally and not in the nicest sense of the word. Camping would be an understatement, these people can plant themselves anywhere they like, disrupting other people's lives, not giving a hoot who they upset of annoy and there's nothing the authorities can do or will do about them. The sad part is, these people, homeless people, have no place to go, and the building owners, shop owners or residents, pay good money to live where they are. It's easy to feel sorry for both, depending on your persuasion, but really, if the city opened more shelters or more places for homeless people to sleep safely, (hard to do without upsetting someone, somewhere), then maybe there would be less friction between those who have and those who don't? Doubtful, but I can always hope. Anyway, the issue with regular homeless people upsetting local people who are trying hard to make a living, leads to friction that you need to witness to believe. I saw one homeless man begging in front of an Asian marketplace. He was being so disruptive that the owner, presumably the owner, I never found out if it was or not, came out of the store brandishing a Samurai sword and threatening to cut this guy's head off if he didn't move to another spot. I could tell from his facial expressions that he was deadly serious, but the homeless man didn't give a fuck, knowing that he had no place else to go and nothing to lose by just sticking to his guns and standing his ground. Chance of being 'executed', in his mind, was zero. Thank goodness the cops intervened before we had to find out who had the stronger will, and the standoff ended peacefully with both aggressor and aggresse moving back into his store and away from the front of the store. Scary to watch, and it happens every day, maybe three to four times a day, not only in that area, but in every area in every city. Maybe not with swords, but often with other weapons, threatening the lives of those who are just trying to get cash or food to stay alive.

Chinatown at 9 AM is filled with trucks delivering goods to stores who are about to open. There are men and women passing through on their way to work, children, some on their way to school, some just hanging around their parents' stores, and some too old to do either. Food is everywhere. Inside and outside, just like most places in America, and it's plentiful. There are stalls, restaurants, kiosks, all with their shelves temptingly laden. It's hard, I suppose, when you're hungry and penniless, to pass by any of these places and not feel the urge just to take what you want. It's all there, out in the open, available and no one is guarding it, no one is really expecting theft of fruit or vegetables, no one except those who own it! They know, they absolutely know, and they care. Each owner watches out for the other. It's like a clique. Protecting their purchased fair is of the utmost importance to all these storekeepers. And, I know from experience, they live in dread, daily, that their produce will be the next to be stolen by the hordes of vagrants who roam their streets by day and by night. When someone who looked like I did that morning, appears in front of their shop-front, they transform immediately into protective mode. I can tell you now, an Asian guy in protective mode is something to fear. Even the older store owners, those over 70, are fearsome. I think it's their culture, their will to survive as immigrants. They take no shit from anyone, and they will give as good as they get. People, who looked like I did that day, are unwelcome by most in this part of San Francisco. My theory was going to be very simple, ask them in Mandarin, their native language, for food or for cash. My looks, Scottish, white and blond, my accent, Scottish of course, and my polite manner, backed up with a few words of Mandarin I've learned on my 40 years plus travel to China, was a sure-fire way to confuse even the fiercest and angriest of all the shop keepers. I was convinced that if I could crack them, I could crack anyone.

My first choice was simple, ask any man in the street, any man who was just walking to wherever his legs were taking him. If I ran out of people to ask, I would move on to the storekeepers.

"Ni Hoa Ma? (how are you)" I asked, as this well-dressed gent walked past me. He stopped, for just a split second and then I hit him with, " wo ele (I'm hungry), qing bangmang, (please help)" That was the extent of my mandarin, other than the few swear words I knew. The man looked at me, and without speaking, decided to move on. 'Oh well,' I thought to myself, 'let's try again'. And then something strange happened. That same man stopped, turned around and came back to me. He thrust a dollar into my hand and without saying a single word, he walked off in the direction he'd started before he'd come back to donate.

What a start! Someone had cared and that made me happy. For the briefest of moments, I wondered how the rest of the gang might be fairing, immediately putting all thought of their progress out of my head and concentrating on my next victim. A lady, yes, a lady, elderly, but very mobile. She looked like she was in a hurry. I tried the same ploy, asking in Mandarin if she could help. She told me in no uncertain terms to "qu ta ma di zjii" which I knew, even from my poor knowledge of her language, meant GO FUCK YOURSELF, spat into my face with pure venom and disdain. I was shocked, although not in the least surprised. I also knew that it wouldn't be the last time someone told me to do that on this particular day.

Time was moving on, my success rate wasn't great and I had to pick up my 'gang at 10.30 ish, although with time on these streets not meaning too much, it wouldn't be a disaster if I arrived later. After all, where else could they go?

Mannequin Pisser

He urinates at great speed
One leg in and one leg out
Braving an onslaught of verbal abuse
Caring not that he desecrates a home
Looking only for relief in a hurry

Obstinate and ignorant though desperate too
Drunk beyond comprehension he signals a truce
Staggering towards that inevitable finale
Pleading to many that necessity had called
Loosing no sleep over an act he will never remember

Flowing like a river until an end became visible
Ruining flowers, carpet and his own reputation
Incomparable performance of a mannequin pisser
Confirming his status as a vandal and a thug
Worshiped by those who wear the same colors

Carried into the sunset by a very long arm indeed
Questioned, charged then released to apologize
Finding disbelief in his actions now that he is sober
Knowing not what to say to the anger that awaits
Consumed totally by his inability to perform as a human being

The thing about walking around Chinatown is, that no matter what time of day it is, it's always cold. The sun never seems to shine on that part of town, and although I describe that chill as being more than just a meteorological issue, the sun also never shines from its inhabitants either. Being used to Hong Kong, mainland China and other parts of Asia where I've traveled extensively, I was used to the way these particular immigrant culture had failed to ingratiate itself on us western know-it-alls. They, as a people have been continually battling an inferiority complex for centuries. This great culture, so amazingly rich in history, so ingratiating, yet so very timid, until intimidated!

The Chinese love my face, simply because it's friendly and non-aggressive. I have been told this for years. I also have a cleft chin, something they find not only amusing, but intriguing too. There have been many times on my various trips to the Orient, when I've been stopped randomly in the street by curiosity seekers, just because of that chin, and there have been many times when people, especially women, have wanted to touch it to make sure it's real! They see it as an asset, a mark of friendship, an ice-breaker of sorts. I began going to China in 1979, at which time very few foreigners had ventured into the mainland itself, with most people choosing to spend their time in Hong Kong, rather than crossing over the border. I had the privilege of being one of the early pioneers when China eventually opened its borders and the first time I went to Guangzhou (Canton in old money), my physical appearance seemed to be the cause of a three-car pile-up, just because of the way I was dressed. They, the locals, would come very close to my face and smell me, touch me and just stand and smile at me. At the time, that was, for me, quite hilarious, but as time moved on and foreign travel to China became more popular, these instances completely ceased. In San Francisco, however, I was always going to be just another homeless person and nothing particularly different to what they'd seen before, other than my chin! Oh yes, that chin gets me in Chinese doors that other chins cannot open.

Two kids walked past me, not giving me a second glance, one was about 8, the other perhaps 6? I think they were on their way to school. I noticed out of the corner of my eye a woman, youngish, definitely Asian, running after them, and really concerned about something these two kids were doing. Obviously at that point, I had no idea what was going on, but something inside me thought that whatever it was, it wasn't good. She seemed to be waving uncontrollably at both of them and as they had their backs turned towards her, the lady's attempt to make them stop, was going unnoticed by everyone, except me. That woman looked distraught, and with the look she had on her face, I reckoned came only trouble.

I turned around and shouted at the kids, one of who looked back at me and smiled, as the other, the older of the two, carried on walking. The younger one seemed intrigued that a stranger wanted to talk to her, whilst the older one was probably following his mother's advice in never speaking to strangers.

"You mother is shouting at you" I said, presuming indeed that this lady was actually their mother, and as I said this, I pointed in the opposite direction to the woman who was trying to catch them up.

The child smiled again, then realized that her sibling was no longer by her side, indeed, he'd walked on about 50 yards and was now waiting for a red pedestrian light to turn green, thus allowing him to cross a busy intersection. The confusion inside my head was confounded tenfold when I realized that the boy at the light was being manhandled by another man, an older man, maybe in his early 40's. This didn't look good and it didn't look right.

I made my mind up in an instant that the boy needed help. The woman, who I now prayed was the mother, had caught up to the little girl and was now on her knees hugging her child.

"Is he in danger?" I asked her, as I pointed to the boy.

"Yes, his daddy is drunk and mad, please help."

The question was, what could I do? I am not a violent person, in fact, I have never been involved any physical altercations in all my years on this earth. She looked desperate. I looked scared.

Without thinking too much about the consequences of what I was about to do, and blessed with amazing sprint capabilities, I took off down that road in a flash, angling, darting, dodging my way through all of the people who were blocking that sidewalk. I raced like crazy to get to the light before it changed to green and before the drunk dad could get his hand on the child. Just like in the movies, although this was real life, I pounced on the child, grabbing him with both arms and pulling him backwards towards me. The father, seeing that I'd reached his kid before him and then realizing I was a homeless person, started shouting out loud.

"Thief! Thief! He stole my child, he stole him!"

The whole street seemed suddenly to stop and look, as this scene unfolded. The mother, who by now was on her feet again and running as quickly as she could carrying her little girl on her body, the girls' arms around her mother's neck and feet around her waist, was catching up to me fast. The dad, who had maneuvered his body and drunken limbs to line up in a perfect match with each other, (that was quite a feat considering the state he was in), looked very angry and very drunk indeed. I knew then, he'd either pull out a machete and chop off my head, or take a step back and hope a fight didn't materialize. The former was out of the question, too many cops patrolled these streets, so I presumed, and it turned out rightly so, I was in for some kind of verbal assault.

"Why you take my son? Who the fuck are you? Why you take my son?" he went on and on and on. The mother caught up to where I was standing with her son. The boy looked shit scared. The father instantly decided to back off and I sensed he feared this woman.

The mother came up to me and grabbed her son. The father ran in the opposite direction. The mother looked at me, nodding her head as if to say 'thank you' and asked me,

"You saved him. That man is mad, I owe you."

"You owe me nothing, I am glad to help. Your son looked scared."
"Yes, he beat him all the time" she said, "he very drunk and stupid" Her English was broken and very Chinese.

"You should get rid of him" I suggested.

"Too expensive. I make all money" she told me.

"OK, well I am glad it worked out."
"You homeless?' she was curious.
"Not really, I am writing a book and am seeing what it's like to live on the streets"
"Here, take!" she said, and as she spoke, she gave me a $20 note. "This was his drink money that I refused to give to him, that's why he was so angry. He run away, mad, after kids, make me mad. You spend it on anything you like"

Then she walked off, two kids in hand, to begin the rest of her day, a day that it seemed could only get better.

Recluse On A Street Named Destiny

Bow tie, untied, soiled and black
Hanging loosely around a neck in need of twisting
Looking sideways, downwards and all over
Hesitating inside shoes that can no longer walk
Confirming his status of recluse
Offering no way out to this, a one-way streak
Nowhere in particular, his destiny
Shamelessly in need of good fortune
Covered in mishaps, he bends to pick up distractions
Each one, a sad reflection of himself
Mirrors, lying beaten and desperate
All, male and female alike, replaceable
Unknowns, except to those they barely know
Condemned to survive, right here, on skid row
Sentence, long and severe, without a finale
Abandonment, the only certainty society has established
This street, like many others, to be avoided
A place where regular people should never be seen dead
Filled with unfortunates who are barely alive

$25 in my pocket and running into serious issues with the rest of the gang. My thoughts focused on how they might be doing. I decided enough was enough and I'd head back to meet them. It was time for a moment of truth and to reveal who'd collected the most cash. I walked slowly back to Market St, and not surprisingly, none of the 4 of my cohorts were anywhere to be seen. They'd all vanished, at least it looked that way. The most incredible fact about looking for someone you know who is a homeless person, they all look the same! Black looks like white and visa versa. It's amazing, when you are part of that particular community, it's hard to differentiate who is who. Standing on Market St that morning, looking out at both street corners where all four were supposed to be hanging out, all I could see were homeless people, dozens of them, although none I recognized and none that belonged to my 'gang'. I kind of panicked, then I took a deep breath, remembering it mattered not if I saw any of them again. I decided to wait. I was early, about 20 minutes early, so I hung out watching the world go by and looking for any opportunity to get some cash from anyone who looked like they might be willing enough to cough it up.

Rob and Bob never came back, and I never saw them again, ever! Fred and Ginger never showed up, but I would meet them again, although under completely different circumstances. It was all so sad to me. They just wanted to be on their own, and my motivation to keep them as a collective had unfortunately failed miserably.

I became very bored standing around for half an hour and thought it best if I made my way to another part of the city. I realized quickly that my 'gang' members had done a runner, and for whatever reason, they weren't coming back. Such a pity, because you need friends when you're on these streets and I believed I had formed a casual bond with all four of them. How wrong I had been.

I had money to get myself home and I was sorely tempted just to make my way to the station and leave town. What more could I achieve? What else would happen in the hours I had left on my journey? A few more dollars wouldn't help, because I also had enough cash for lunch, and dinner would be provided by the shelter, where I intended to sleep once again. So, really, what on earth was I doing here on my own. I could indeed call it a day and march straight home, arriving by early afternoon and showering and going to sleep in a large comfortable bed, where I thought I would stay for at least a day to a day and a half without moving a muscle. My conscience was driving me to stay, my legs were pushing me towards my home. I was very torn.

"Hey you! Scotsman!" came the call.

"WTF??" I turned around and there was Stevie from the shelter, with his wife or girlfriend.

"Where are you going?" he asked.

"Well," I replied, "I was torn between ending my homelessness right here and heading to the train station, or hanging around for one more night, just like I promised myself I'd do. My friends have deserted me, and I'm not sure I can tolerate another day of just faking it." "Listen," Stevie said, "We are on our way back to the shelter, this is Annie, she's my girlfriend." Annie acknowledged me with a nod of her head, and I could tell she didn't know I was a fake by the way she quickly turned her head in a different direction, avoiding eye contact.

"We are expecting a huge number of people tonight for meal service. Annie is coming to help too. I know we're short of volunteers and it's funny, I was just telling her about you and how mad you are for doing this. So why not come back and help out tonight. You're really needed."

So, she did know!! That thought made her previous reaction to me even stranger. Well, I had nothing else to do, other than walk, so I agreed to go with them. The 3 of us walked off towards the shelter, with Stevie telling Annie about my book and my passion for creating a better environment for anyone who was or was destined to become homeless. Annie warmed up to me quickly.

Back at the shelter I was put to work immediately. Stevie suggested I clean the dining area to get it ready for the evening meal service, and I was happy to do so. Down on my knees, I began scrubbing the floor around the serving area and then I moved to the counter tops. By the time I'd finished, it was almost 2 PM, and I was starving. I marched back to Stevie's office and asked him if he'd mind that I went to get something to eat.

"You do whatever you want" he told me, "Remember, you are volunteering and I have no say on whether you come or go, but also know that we really appreciate you. Do you have money?" And as he asked that question, he realized immediately that he was asking a stupid question. Of course, I had money, and Stevie knew from the stories I'd told him that money was the least of my issues. Still, it was nice of him to ask, and his concern was appreciated. I let him know in no uncertain terms that I appreciated him too. It had become a love fest of sorts and Stevie and I had become big buddies. It's such a shame that two years later, having kept in touch with him over that period of time, asking him continuously if he needed help, money or just support, that Stevie passed away in a car accident. Stevie, you are sorely missed.

Back on Market St and with a spare $35 in my pocket, excluding the train fare for the following day's journey back to San Jose, I wanted to go and eat somewhere decent and not just at any old fast-food place, like Micky Ds or Carl's

Jnr. It was time to eat something that was healthier and more nutritious than I'd had over the past 6 days. Although the food at the shelter had been decent, it hadn't been that great, and as appreciated as it might have been. My old self was now dying to eat something freshly prepared to order. I marched down to this Italian café, just off of Market and decided to go in and order food to take away. Then, just outside the café door, I was suddenly hit by two thoughts.

1 I was dressed and looked like a homeless person.

2 The money I was about to selfishly waste on myself could go to a better cause. Another hungrier homeless being.

I stopped cold and realized I was becoming a true fraud, unintentionally of course, but a fraud indeed. I pulled back from opening the café door, and turned around and retraced my steps back to the shelter. A burger from the $1 menu at Micky Ds would be fine and the rest of my cash I would donate to someone who was more in need of it than I was at that point in time. After all, the following day I could get back to eating what I wanted when I was in the comfort of my own home. The sacrifice was worthwhile.

My burger was delicious, although it vanished in moments, realizing at that point in time I was starving from all the walking and scrubbing I'd done at the shelter. I wanted so badly to purchase another and wash both down with a Coke, but again, my conscience got the better of me, and after asking for a free cup of water, I left the store with my stomach a little happier and my conscience still intact.

On the way back to assist with dinner service at the shelter, I bumped into an elderly lady, one I'd seen before, but someone I'd not spoken to. She too was homeless. I recognized her from the 5 or 6 times I'd passed her in the street and I'd also bumped into her at the shelter, although I couldn't recall if it was the first or second shelter. She was slumped at a street corner holding out her sign, which read something like,

Desperate

Please help, God Bless

It was handwritten in black marker pen, scrawled over a cardboard box top, and held out with little conviction. She looked destitute, beaten by her thankless task and ready to die. I can't imagine how she felt, but really, without any cash in the little jar she'd laid out in front of her and looking like she'd not bathed in years, I decided to stop and see if she'd talk to me, perhaps hoping that if I could get her to chat, I would then get her to join me at the shelter and get herself washed and cleaned.

"Hello darling" I began.

She looked at me from her position, sat on the side walk, and gave me the oddest look, which bordered on both disdain and hatred.

"Are you doing OK?" I persisted

She growled back at me, opening her mouth and sounding like a lioness. I laughed, and that made her even madder.

"Listen," I said, "I'm not here to steal from you or to interfere with what you're doing, but I do have some cash that I would like to give you, and I want to sit and talk to you for a few minutes, if you'd let me?" She was raging now, and ready to kill me. I could just tell by the look on her face and her eyes, which were not evil, they were just filled by rage, years of it.

"Calm down and relax, I promise I am not going to harm you in any way." I said, as I took a $20 bill from my pocket and handed it over to her. Like a tiger, she grabbed it so quickly and in one single movement took it from my outstretched hand and put it straight into an inside pocket of her coat. It was as if she'd practiced that movement for years, just to perfect it, and boy, was it smooth and deliberate! I was totally impressed and this lady was shaping up to be someone not to be messed with. How looks could be deceiving, especially amongst the homeless.

"So, can we talk?" I sounded like I was begging her to chat, but she didn't care, she knew she was in charge.

"Sit!" she commanded.

I did as I was told.

Lady With Backpack And Voice

Through her nose, and out of her mouth
Distorted by volume and angst
Nerves, playing a large part in this, her big day out
Dressed with her backpack as an accessory to be proud of

She lifts her tone to suit her pose
She makes it clear that this, is her day
Calling over her chaperone, her friend
Annoying, though loving, she is in her heaven

Nasal expressions funnel slowly into cold fresh air
Some out loud, some so quietly, others, in silence
Feeling her way into a situation, obviously unfamiliar
Pressing her point of view, childish for one her age, without confusion

Soon to disappear into that darkness that spells entertainment
A loss to the color of a square, now in silence
Festive sweater, festive spirit, gone for another year
A character to remember, just like her enthusiasm and naiveté

Nora, her name was Nora. She was 72, although she looked like she was 95. She'd been homeless for 23 years, all stemming from a fight she'd had with her husband at the time. He'd kicked her out, kicked her and the kids out, and he'd gambled away their home, cars and bank accounts. Her route to desolation had been compounded by her loss of her two children, both murdered, both in their early 20's and both killed in separate incidents in different cities, two weeks apart. Nora was a powerful example of our entire system gone wrong, and a victim of abuse, both physical and mental, that had destroyed her entire life and placed her on these streets, streets that she'd never managed to escape. Nora was bitter, very bitter, and no wonder. She'd been raped, beaten, and stood upon for years, and not just once, many times, but she'd survived and she'd become the person with whom I was now talking to, interesting, quite humorous, in her own way and very cautious of anyone who wanted to look inside her past. I came clean with Nora, letting her know what my real intentions had been and that my book, should it ever get published, would certainly highlight the plight of people just like her. She asked me if she would be mentioned in the book and I promised her that she would. I am sure, since it was 15 years ago, Nora is no longer with us, but as promised, this little space, filled with words that perhaps describe this brave lady, will suffice in keeping that promise. Nora, you opened my eyes. You are one of the bravest people I have ever met in my life. I was so grateful to you for sitting with me, even if it was only for a few minutes, that afternoon and I have no idea how you survived all those years living on the streets of San Francisco, without family, without friends and always without hope. I will always remember you.

Nora also told me about her fight, daily fight, with her own demons, demons that pushed her to jump off the Golden Gate Bridge and just end her misery. Demons that carried her close to suicide every day and demons that kept her wake for days on end, hoping that someone would just put an end to the distress she endured each and every day. Nora, yes, a singer, at one point in her life, a talented performer, and probably a very sweet endearing lady, now relegated to sitting on street corners, begging for food, hoping for an end to all of her destitution. An end that would probably never come, and probably never did.

As I got up to leave, I gave her another $10 and I promised myself I would drive back to the city one day and find her, give her more money and more of everything she needed to get out of this dreadful situation. I never did, and sadly, I have no idea what happened to her. I hope, if she's still alive, she is being taken care of, because she'd be in her 80's by now. If she'd dead, and chances are strong that's the case, then I hope she's at peace and will now rest into all eternity.

Nora!

Nora

Beneath your anxiety there lies humanity
A version of you that no one remembers
Hidden for years, exposed for the very few
I, the lucky one, found you wanting
Offering more than just solace, I made you whole
If only for moments, if only for the briefest of seconds
We found a common ground and hope

Nora, you have been deserted by all who cared
Vanished into a world, so cruel
Taken from you, everything so dear, so perfect
Ending up dying in a prison called homelessness
Reflecting daily on how to end your misery
You are brave, you are strong, you are special
Your soul, left inside my heart, now spread upon this page

Dinner service ended, and I thought to myself, "I did it! I actually did it!! I survived a week" Then I sat down and asked myself, 'did I really achieve anything?'

My heart was pounding and I clearly recall looking around the dining area of that shelter realizing that I was so fortunate, so blessed and yet, so incredibly sad for everyone else in that room who seemed condemned. They had little chance of escaping their misfortune, whereas I was on my way home to another life, a life most of these people would never experience again, if indeed they ever had. It's frustrating to note that there is so much wealth in the USA and also so much poverty. Some might say, "that's life!", whereas others will take a completely different approach and dedicate their entire existence to making sure this discrepancy, the difference between the haves and the have not's, is eliminated and a certain amount of fairness is introduced into a world that has so obviously never been fair. The chances of the latter ever happening, in my opinion, is none to zero. Life is lived by 99.9% of our population, in the most selfish of ways. My beliefs, specifically when asking myself, 'why am I here?', is that we exist to help those who are less fortunate than ourselves. We are here for that purpose and that purpose only. Yes, you can buy status in life, you can purchase fancy clothes, cars, and other toys. Yes, you can eat the best food, live your best life and enjoy every minute of it, but unless you give back, what use have you been to anyone in society, other than yourself? Giving back, assisting other people, making a difference, no matter how small, no matter to how few, well, THAT makes life all the more worthwhile. Again, these are my opinions and I don't expect agreement from everyone as to whether my intentions or beliefs are correct or not. In the end, we all die, no one survives. In that case, why are we all so intent on grabbing as much as we can, and so much more than we really need, when, after death, we leave it all behind and cannot take it with us?

The shelter was a complete grounding for me where even life's basics weren't available to those who wanted them. This was a makeshift attempt by some of us who care to make life a little less difficult for people who have nothing. And my next question was, 'where would these homeless people be without the efforts and sacrifice from those who have made the decision to assist?'

God only knows what would happen if there were no shelters, no volunteers, no donations of food and clothing, no medical assistance, no nothing! 2 million plus homeless people would perish, a slow and needlessly desperate death. I advocate for change, I plead with everyone to reconsider their stance on this problem, this pandemic, which isn't just here in the USA, it's a world-wide problem. Ask any government how they are treating this issue in their own countries? They're all the same, throwing money and hollow promises at an issue that is only getting worse. I have traveled the planet, and there are homeless people everywhere. I don't think I have ever been to a country or a city where homelessness doesn't exist. Have you? Later in the book I will give you some examples of humorous homeless stories I've experienced myself, but in general, homelessness isn't funny. It's a genuine problem and to witness it first-hand, to live it for a week, to assist on a regular basis in shelters that cater to these people, is to experience the worst depravity that life has to offer and it makes one think, 'how on earth did we let this happen?'

Drugs play a huge part of every-day life amongst our homeless communities and although the average age of those on the streets has increased over the past few years, I believe the median age in 2022 is now 32, the issues relating to drug abuse, drug usage, and drug dependency has also increased. All or most of our government programs to combat the issues of drug abuse and mental health, as I mentioned earlier in the book, are no longer available, or if they are available, they are working on reduced budget and capacities and cannot cope with the influx of new addicts or people who are mentally unfit. It's a sad fact that profit has come before assistance, but then again, that's the society we now live in and I fear that it's only going to get worse.

So, as I sat, looking at all these people, who made up a very small fraction of the true problem walking around outside on the streets of San Francisco, I wondered, 'how the hell am I going to make a difference?'

Scruffy On A Bike

He hadn't washed for a year, at least
Scruffy, they called him Scruffy
Peddling on his bike to nowhere in particular
Up and down the same road at the same times
Moving slowly, stopping regularly
Emptying trash from empty lives
His passion or perhaps just his need

Clothes that could be smelt from a great distance
Ragged and dirty in the heat of today
Grey, dull and definitely not his size
Procured by scavenging his friendly neighborhood
Donated, though not at will, by so called rich folk
Accepted gratefully and never changed
Sticking to his flesh like glue

Sometimes a smile appeared from behind his beard
Wry, to say the least
Hovering there, in the middle of nowhere
Baring yellow teeth and his famous alcoholic breath
Showing his thanks in the shape of chapped lips
Moving onwards to repeat his sad journey
Followed by eyes, delighted to see him disappear

I couldn't sleep that night. I was too excited about going home. In fact, I was so close to just calling it quits and leaving, but decided it would be best to say my goodbyes to Stevie and his crew the following morning, so I stuck it out. That night went on and on and on. Each minute seeming like an hour, and each hour like a whole day. I never had a watch on my wrist, in fact I never wear one, but looking around and counting down the minutes until dawn in desperate need of relief from the surrounding misery, drove me to complete distraction. I was done, and I never wanted to ever come back. I wanted a shower, a shit in a proper clean toilet and a shave. I hated my puny attempt at growing a beard, although I realized it had been a necessary part of my disguise. After all, who ever saw a clean shaved homeless person before? Anyway, after much contemplation, walking back and forth in and out of the dorm, I settled down and must have fallen asleep for an hour or so because I remember clearly at 6 AM, an African American man standing over me, touching my feet and muttering some indistinguishable babble from his frothy mouth. It scared the crap out of me, until I realized that what he was after was my coat and my blanket. I had mentioned to a few guys at dinner the previous evening that I intended to get on my way and leave the shelter and make for pastures new. Of course, in that sense, no one knew if I was being housed or just making my way to a different part of town or even a new city. News travels fast, and Mr. African American took it upon himself to be the first in line for any cast off's I might decide to discard.

"Fuck off Jimmy!" I shouted. It wasn't really a shout, more of a command. The froth coming from his mouth suddenly ceased and he backed the fuck away, faster than a greyhound chasing a rabbit around a track. I realized there and then that I was done. I got up, went into Stevie's office, wrote him a note and left the building. It was 6.28 AM, and I will never forget the relief as I exited into the street and made my way towards the BART station which would take me back to the train station and a safe passage back to San Jose and home. I was full of the joys of spring, and enjoying every moment of my realization that I was no longer a homeless being, I was a free-bird and ready to carry on my life with the same intensity I had before I'd come up to the city a week ago. I was re-born, I was joyous and I was smelly! Obviously I had enough cash to get me home, using the money I'd saved to purchase a ticket all the way back to where I'd begun this journey. My inherent belief was that I would never come up to San Francisco again. I'd had enough, I'd seen the best and really the worst of humanity. I never wanted to experience any of this again and not coming back to the city seemed like the best way of avoiding it and curbing all of my fears and anxiety. That thought, however, didn't last long. Shortly after, about 6 weeks later, I found myself back in San Francisco on another mission, but, that's a story for another day. On this particular morning, all I was interested in doing was returning to my real life and sleeping, perhaps for days.

My journey home took less than 2 hours from beginning to end and on that train journey, I sat, pensive, full of praise for those who I'd met and those who had to remain in a state of homelessness. Those who helped and those who volunteered. Those who were condemned to a whole life of misery and obviously those who had made an everlasting impression on my soul, some for the right reasons, but many for the wrong. Those wrong impressions had come from both sides of the fence. Some who were not homeless and some who were. It didn't matter in life, there was always going to be good and bad in every sector, but perhaps the good outweighed the bad? Who knows? All I knew at that point in time was that I needed to put all my thoughts down in writing, write this book and then have it published, in order to raise funds and awareness for everyone's plight. I am just sorry it's taken me so long to get round to finishing it off. I began the process of writing Cardboard City, many years ago, starting and stopping several times. Most of what I had written prior to this attempt had been total crap, and then, after writing two other novels, both true, The Secret Masseuse and the Secret Escort, when Covid hit, it gave me the opportunity to really get into the nuts and bolts of Cardboard City and once and for all get it down in a format that I hope is entertaining and informative. My poetry, intermingled between accounts of my journey, has been amassed over a period of 25 years. The poems include accounts of scenes I have witnessed all over the world in my life on this planet, some current, some when I was so much younger, but all true and all witnessed first-hand and then transcribed into words that are, well, meaningful to me and hopefully to you too. I have seen a lot in my life, maybe not as much as some of you out there, but a lot nonetheless. My life has been blessed with so much goodness and warmth, love and understanding, perhaps more than I have ever deserved, but when I think back to that week, the week I left it all behind and took a chance, perhaps and idiotic chance, on being homeless, just to experience the trials and tribulations of life on skid row, rather than Saville Row, it taught me one thing in particular and one thing I will take with me to my grave.

We are all human, every single one of us. Not one of us, that we know of has ever died anywhere other than planet earth. So, if that's the case, what the heck are we all fighting over? We cannot go anywhere, other than here, and we cannot die anyplace other than here, well, not yet, and I have to ask the question, why are we not helping each other instead of continually fighting with one another? It makes no sense. But then again, has anything on this planet ever made sense?

My train pulled into the station near my home, and I got off. The platform, never crowded no matter what time of day, was pretty empty, although some of the looks that I received from those who were standing waiting to board, were those of complete disgust. I wanted to shout out, "I AM NOT HOMELESS", but I didn't, trying to ignore the stress and move forward towards the exit, where, I would leave the station and make the short walk back to my home. It took about 30 minutes to get there and when the front door opened, I rushed into the bathroom, took out my shaver, turned on the shower and prepared to return to the Alan that everyone knew. After cleaning up, throwing the clothes I'd been wearing for a week into the garbage and putting on my clean tee shirt and shorts, I lay down on my bed, thinking only of the people I'd left in San Francisco, not with any regret, but more with pity. There was absolutely nothing about my time up there that I would ever miss, but the thought of all of those who were still there, living rough, day to day, weighed heavily on my mind, as I tried hard to close my eyes and fall asleep. I must have dozed off, because about 7 hours later, I awoke and it was evening. I couldn't believe it. I wasn't hungry, I was exhausted. I lay in bed, drifting off again in to dreamland. Finally, around 4 Am the following morning, I got up, making myself some breakfast and heading to my gym. The gym was never that busy at 5 AM when it opened, but as a regular attendee at that hour, there was a select group who got to know one another, the diehards, always there right before the doors opened, ready and willing to sacrifice every ounce of effort to remain trim, fit and healthy, all in the name of self-preservation and vanity. Having been away for a week and having never told anyone where I was going or what I was doing, I was accosted in the parking lot by several of the guys who I knew well. "Slacker!"

"Lazy fuck"

"We don't take days off"

Just some of the comments that came my way, all in good nature of course.

"I was out of town fuckers! Did you miss me?" I replied, and with that, the doors opened, and my life just returned to its normal path, as if nothing had ever happened or nothing ever would.

Not Jesus

Jesus he is not
A once great man
Lying on a doorstep of benevolence
Looking for a miracle
Finding little sacrifice
Warmed only by thoughts of his past
Resting against his world
Lost in a life that never was

Prayer and forgiveness
His only similarity, other than his beard
Disciples, gone, run far from here
Unable to partake in any further contact
Eating daily, his last supper
Drinking from that same cup
Filled but never brimming
Cheap wine, irrelevant but necessary

Abandoned by all who once believed
Only the brave now come calling
Irregular with visits that last but moments
Feeling uncomfortable inside the gaze of a dropout
Preferring to hide behind their lap of luxury
Limiting contact for fear of embarrassment
Finding many excuses to remain aloof
Monsters that once were true friends

Slumped by the cross at the end of his journey
Nailed to streets that have become so cruel
Asking his Lord for an end to this madness
Receiving little, taking less
Certain that someplace an angel lurks
Ready and willing to end this misery
Staring death in its all-out glory
An inevitability that will bring well-earned peace

I thought it might be interesting to recount some of the more humorous stories from my years dealing with homeless people and working in homeless shelters. One or two are funny and worth repeating. It's not all doom and gloom out there, even though the doom and gloom far outweigh anything positive that might happen in the jungle-like conditions that involves walking those lonely streets.

My office in London, when I lived in that particular city, was surrounded by homeless people. I moved to London when I was 18, living in the Regents Park area of the city, right across the road from the Regents Park Zoo, one of London's major tourist attractions. I think the homeless population gathered there just because of the number of tourists they had to feed off. I used to walk from my office/home to Camden Town underground (tube) station on a regular basis, to go to meetings in central London. It was at that time that I began to take a serious interest in the vagrants who roamed around that area and, as I seemed to see basically the same people, male and female, all the time, we kind of had a rapport. I would nod to them, and they would nod back, which progressed into bidding one another an occasional "good morning", and then into the, "why did you end up here?", conversation. It was quite interesting for me in many ways. I rarely, if ever, gave them any money, but that's another story, and I never ever saw any of them doing drugs, asking for drugs or telling me they needed drugs to get through their days. This was 1978, so perhaps a different era from present day, but most of the same crap went on, minus the drugs. Or maybe I was just too young and innocent to realize they were all addicted? Alcohol though, seemed to be the drug of choice back then and the number of times I was asked to go into a store and buy whoever was requesting, a bottle of cheap vodka or wine, was, extraordinary. At first, I hated the fact they were even asking, but as I grew up, and their requests grew old, I began to stand up to them, often shouting back, "give it up you moron, you're killing yourself". These people rarely took advantage of me and even though I was always smartly dressed in a suit and tie, they understood that the world separated us through choice. In those days, most of the homeless people were there because they wanted to be. Those who did not wish to be on the streets but found themselves there anyway, were mainly ex-military people who had severe mental issues form their days serving our country, and unfortunately could not find their calling in society and had just dropped off the grid. I was very friendly with our local constabulary too. Most of the regular police in London at that time were great people and worthy of conversation and friendship, plodding their 'beat' (streets), and going to great pains to befriend their communities, something that again, doesn't happen in 2022, not in the UK and certainly not here, in the US. Cops are seen to be the bad guys, only driving cars, never interacting with their communities, something I vehemently disagree with. Police are the heart and soul of a community and interaction with the public is so important, and at that time, in London, even the most vicious members of the local communities were respected and treated with some kind of honesty and respect by the 'old bill' (police). There were no guns either, and that made a huge difference. Anyway, I built friendships with the homeless and the police, I was becoming well-known to both sides and over time I was introduced to people who assisted the homeless and also to causes/charities who tried to raise money to get those who were homeless, off the streets. Neither were effective in any way shape or form, and the problems just got worse as the years went by. I moved out of that area after spending 5 years there and the next area of London I moved to, just about 3 miles from Regents Park, had its homeless issues too. I used to meet homeless people daily, morning noon and night and often I would give them money to go and buy food or alcohol. Yes, I hadn't learned at that point in my life that it wasn't a sensible move to give them cash. One evening, I remember it was dark, so it must have been winter time, and it was only 4 or 5 PM, I was walking out of my office and around the corner to get in my car to drive to the south of London. I walked about 50 yards and there was a guy propped up against a fence. The fence was the front of someone's home, but he was slumped against it, the top half of his body and his back, balanced on the bars of the fence and his legs, spread out into the street. I knew from the moment I set eyes on him that he was homeless and I also knew, from experience, that he was about to ask me for money. I preempted that request by taking some cash out of my pocket, all the time thinking, 'this guy looks in real trouble so no matter what, I'll give him something"

I walked up to him; my car was parked almost opposite where he was sitting.

"Hello Boss, how are you? Here's a fiver (five pounds), go get yourself something to eat."

"It's OK mate" he replied, "I don't want it."

"No, seriously, go buy yourself some food or a drink" I insisted.

"No thanks, I am fine" he replied.

As I thrust the money into his space, my hand and arm coming within inches of his face, I said, "well at least get yourself a bath and some shelter."

I dropped the 5 pounds onto his outstretched legs and began to walk away.

"Mate" he said, as he stood up and threw the money back at me, "will you just leave me alone. I am sitting here waiting for my wife!"

He wasn't homeless after all! I was so embarrassed. I never did that again and was always very careful who I approached before offering to give money.

And then there was a time outside Starbucks in Portland, Oregon. I was walking towards a restaurant, when a homeless guy came out of Starbucks shouting and screaming,

"They're going to kill me; they're going to kill me!!!" at the top of his voice. Everyone on the street was watching and listening, but this guy kept on shouting, "They're going to kill me, they're going to kill me!" Unfortunately, I was in his direct path of retreat. He approached me and shouted, right in my face, "They're going to kill me, they're going to kill me!!!"

I shoved him back, using the force of both my arms, pushing them into his stomach and replied, "If they're going to kill you, don't stand next to me!" The whole street laughed. The homeless guy also saw the funny side of it and he stopped shouting. The Starbucks staff came outside and gave him free food and drink, but the poor guy was mentally unfit to be anywhere other than in a hospital somewhere. What a shame.

Also in Portland Oregon, there's a river walk which runs along the Columbia River, a river which splits the town into north and south. There are 20 plus bridges that cross that river but the south side has a huge grass bank that follows most of that walking path. One afternoon, it was boiling hot, there was a homeless guy placing sticks into certain areas of the grass bank. These sticks were tall and thin and he had about ten of them. I became curious and stopped to watch. He placed the sticks strategically all along that bank and then went back towards his 'stash' or 'belongings', where he proceeded to take out a tennis ball and then he sat down with two branches from a tree. He took out some string from a bag, tied the two branches together in a kind of L-shape, mimicking the shape of a golf club and then proceeded to play golf with the branches and tennis ball, hitting that ball towards each stick he'd placed in the ground. This went on for 45 minutes after which he was joined by two other homeless people, both in their early 30's. "Right," he shouted towards them, "I've warmed up, let's play!"

And they did. The three of them played exactly 18 hoes, keeping score, taking penalty shots and drinking beers in between breaks in the game. It was hilarious to watch until the end, when the original guy accused one of the others of cheating and a full-on fight blew up in front of me and some other people who'd stopped to watch, after taking an interest in this game. Police intervention put an end to the fight and all three were reprimanded by the cops and told not to do it again., The cops confiscated the 'golf club' much to the annoyance of the homeless guy who'd put it together, telling him that if they ever caught him playing on this 'course' again, he'd be jailed.

I wrote about that man, a poem I am very proud of, and it follows below.

Driver

L-shaped and tied
Bound by clothing
Twigs, perhaps a branch
Held by hands of steel
A driver, HIS driver
Ready and waiting to tee off
Watched by the usual crowd
Flapping restlessly as play began
Unable to cheer
Sensing only tension
Stepping back in awe, but with no applause

Directly into the middle
Sending his yellow ball skywards
Aim, perfect
Just a little fade
Put there deliberately
Sitting nicely in the center of his fairway
Marching with some pride towards an easy second
Taking care to scout out his shot
Leaving no room for error
Practicing then once again, making it count
Delighted by a direct hit

With arms raised high, he took his bow
Seeing nothing other than fame in his next fifteen minutes
Hardly nervous, just happy
Sinking one more on his round to nowhere
Looking towards heaven as that six-footer was sunk
Bagging his twig
Picking up his trusted ball
Leaving for that next tee
Amazed that no offer had yet been made
Counting the prize money, he had yet to win
Disappearing back into the open space that was now home

I thought I'd seen it all until I went to Venice Beach a few weeks back. I used to live close by Marina Del Ray, a suburb of LA, and walk from there to Venice, every Sunday, which was quite a trek. I did this, religiously from 1992 to 1993, loving every minute of every step, and thanking God that I had moved to Southern California from the UK. The walk was amazing, with the Pacific Ocean on my right as I walked south and then on my left as I walked back north to my car. The opposite side to the beach was also interesting. The shops, eclectic and familiar and the fresh breeze coming from the ocean, wafting the smells of BBQ, bakeries and other great restaurants, way up into the air, enhancing each step and spurring on my often-tired legs. Onwards and upwards, as each mile passed by effortlessly. There were also amazing 'people watching', experiences to be found and very few 'beach bums' or homeless to be seen. 30 years later, that same walk is now decorated ONLY by the homeless. Filling up both sides of Pacific Coast Highway with disgustingly filthy tented villages, drug and disease-ridden and occupied by over 45,000 people claiming refuge in what were once, beautiful neighborhoods. It's disgusting to see and disgraceful that we have allowed this to happen. This is not the main problem though, here in LA. The downtown area of Los Angeles can boast even more homeless people than Venice Beach, living in even more disgusting ways, if that's humanly possible, than their counterparts in the west of the city. It's completely out of control and even though the local authorities claim to be doing something about this problem, nothing is changing and it's getting worse by the day. Hollywood is infested by the dregs of life. Dotted around multi-million-dollar homes, are the disgusting, the distraught, the down trodden, the druggies, the worst of all humanity, and yet, we are doing too little to help them and therefore help the destiny of our cities. This process is being repeated all over America, all over the world, and it's completely out of control and totally unacceptable. Admittedly, some, although not the majority, of these people living on our streets, are doing so because it suits them, and in some cases, they are being paid to live there. There are plenty of examples of those who are genuinely homeless and those who boast being fake homeless people that you can find on the internet. We have the radicals, out there to cause trouble and live off handouts from Government programs while they cause trouble in our streets, and there are those who really need those handouts but aren't getting them. We need to try to weed out the bad from the good, but all too often it's easier just to lump everyone into the same category, making it survival of the fittest, or the most radical.

What can you do to help?

There are many things that we, the general public could do to help.

1. Find yourself a volunteer position at one of your local shelters or homeless organizations.

2. DO NOT give cash to homeless people you meet or who accost you in the streets. Offer them food, shelter, a bath, clothing, but never cash. Cash is so often misused and squandered on bad habits, such as drugs, alcohol, and the likes.

3. Campaign at local government level for more programs to assist those who have real mental issues.

4. Clean up our streets and let's find a way to remove homeless people from street corners, beaches, parks and make out cities safe again, enabling our children to go outside without fear of being accosted.

Simply put, if the swell from grass roots level, you and I being those roots, doesn't bring change, the mess we currently live under will only get worse. Disease will increase, crime will increase and the demolition of all that was once so beautiful in our country will just vanish under a sea of humanity with no place else to go.

Homelessness should be our number one concern in the United States. Without a reversal in this current trend of more and more people joining the ranks of those who live on our street corners, we are surely going to end up in a society overwhelmed by poverty and starvation, or, perhaps we are already there?

As with all my other books, any proceeds from sales are donated to specific charities relating to the subject matter of that book. My book **Kennel Hill**, about dogs, raised funds for animal shelters, my other two books, **The Secret Masseuse**, and **The Secret Escort** were written for the sole purpose of raising awareness and funds to prevent sex trafficking in the USA. This book, **Cardboard City**, as you now know will have all of its profits donated to worthy charities who support the homeless cause.

If you or anyone you know run such a charity and would like to be considered as a recipient of any funds raised from the sales of this book, please get in touch with me through the contact form on my web site, www.alanzoltie.com

Road to Paradise

This is not the road to paradise
Watching tears roll from those big blue eyes
With a smile that makes a poor disguise
This is not the road to paradise

Looking through those doors of little hope
Seeing faces that can hardly cope
Holding hands with ones they love and trust
Leaving soon becomes their only must

With a needle poked into a heart
Looking forward to a brand new start
There's a rainbow and it's not too far
Pot of gold that hangs upon a star

This is not the road to paradise
Only eight years old, he sits and cries
Giving praise and telling small white lies
This is not the road to paradise

Many months go by while fighting hard
Strong in mind but with a heart that's scarred
Showing all how brave this man can be
Just a boy who wants the world to see

Believers come from his great energy
Knowing chance is not what it seems to be
Hanging on to every word he speaks
And the new beginnings that he seeks

This is not the road to paradise
Slow and certain in his sad demise
Looking forwards to a nice surprise
This is not the road to paradise

Each and every day they leave him there
Not a wave but more a goodbye stare
Returning back again for more remorse
Watching poison running out its course

Sensing this may be that final chance
Holding hands together in a distant trance
Only one son on his way to pass
Oh so slowly with no pain at last
This is not the road to paradise
Watching tears roll from those big blue eyes
With a smile that makes a poor disguise
This is not the road to paradise

And for a finale, here are just a few of the hundreds of poems I've written over the years that depict some of the experiences and encounters I have witnessed first-hand. I hope they bring to life, in your mind, how incredible desperate these people are and how completely insane our society has become that we've allowed this to happen in such an outrageous and unforgivable manner. There will be many more of these poems on my web site, alanzoltie.com, in the future.

Wheels On The Bus

The wheels on the bus go round and round
Watched silently by Joe
Stuck to the ground alongside his fence
Condemned for life
Unable to pay that fare
Waving relentlessly to a driver who is blind

Smiling with some hope, he gazes
Mesmerized by speed and distance
Wishing for one chance
Knowing his opportunity was now long gone
Sensing perhaps that one day he would receive a response
But the wheels on that bus kept moving

How hard he tries to be noticed
Jumping without moving, moving without jumping
Paralyzed to the spot where he was left
Entertainment for some, ridicule for others
Happy amongst the scenery he knows
Backdrop to a world that will always pass him by

Unfortunate Trilogy

Part 1- Janice

Janice was a whore
A slut
A lady of the night
Playing many tricks
Spending her wasted life needlessly
Using sex as a means to survive

Janice was young
Too young
Getting old too quickly
Learning to survive on dead beats
Unable to escape
Trapped by a pimp named Mark

Janice was cute
No longer so
Scarred by experience
Marked from top to bottom
Made up for improvement
Not yet twenty five

Janice had a degree
Micro Biology
Never used other than to cure her pain
Tempted by money
Deceived by most
Janice was now a corpse

Part 2-Mark

Mark was a pimp
Not just one but sixteen
A stable of willingness
Searching for a new life
Never able to progress
Under the ward of a true pro

He made his cut
Maybe more than just chump change
Keeping in line those who failed to perform
Seeking a little which meant a lot
Never violent, only abusive
Packing a weapon, but not between his legs

She came in hope
He came with force
Free as a test for all who were to pay
Hiring a service he knew would profit
Leaving the rest to a woman in need
Sending a rookie to do the job of a veteran

The news came hard
Hitting home where the door was opened
Taking flight for pastures new
Remembering only her willingness
Forgetting her tender age
Realizing that Janice was now a corpse

Part 3- Bobby

Bobby was a cop
Seen it all before and then once again
Quiet, unassuming, until that badge shone bright
Run ragged from case to case
Vice, worked with energy and patience
Seeking more than just leads and clues

This wouldn't be his first or his last
Strewn, legs apart, naked
A yellow outline depicting a former life
Taken in a brief moment of rage
Pointless in the progression of humanity
Bringing anger and pity and yet more work

Longing for just one more cup of blackness
Seeing those eyes, open and scared
Silent in thought though active in solution
Making haste for conclusion and satisfaction
Spurred on by one thing alone
Her age and that look of desperation

He knew her pimp, Mark was his name
Incapable, or so he thought, of mutilation
Inquisitive methods revealing more
Onward towards yet another arrest
Successful yet unhappy in one particular thought
Janice was still a corpse.

Sun Burnt Life

Scars on the last legs of a journey never completed
Burnt, though not beyond recognition
Watched by many, helped by none
Seemingly tired of her seat amongst disbelievers
Eyes that show fear, now bleeding tears
Covering her head, she bows in favor of another direction

A scarf to hide embarrassment, now a blindfold
Placed sparingly upon a red raw face
Weather beaten in the name of survival
Ageing and tired, like the soul beneath those rags
Propped up against a bench waiting for assistance
Certain that the rest of her days would be as helpless as now

With many blisters and even more scars
A sad smile, just momentarily, breaking her misery
Looking hopefully into the eyes of a donor
Pleading for small donations to an ever-worthy cause
Receiving blank stares in return
Not the cure she desperately requires to fix her sun burnt life

Street in China

A young man, perhaps ten or eleven, dirty, very dirty
Staring amiably at a western face
Strangers for all time, but never a day longer
Passing quickly along a street somewhere in China
Surrounded by a circus that has become every day life
Prison cell to billions who know only barriers
Trapped amongst dereliction and madness
Unable to go anywhere other than home

Two young ladies, one pregnant, the other with child, stopped dead
Balloons, from a nearby school, settling gently against yesterday's trash pile
Drunken workers forming a line, but not a straight one
All with one thing in common
All with a desire to be heard
Remaining calm, though frustrated as wealth passes by in a van
Gone, into the distance, for at least that day
Returning frequently to continue, behind the barrier they now rest upon

A shout, a call and sometimes a scream
Barking dogs fighting for scraps that belong to the hungry
Schools emptying their bowls into the jaws of the wicked
Bicyclists, by the hundred, unaware of any traffic laws
Finding civility in the sound of a car horn
Ringing bells that can be heard only by guardian angels
Weaving endlessly through this plague called humanity
Arriving to nowhere in particular, their terminus to reality

As rivers run through concrete jungles and ceaseless noise
continues unabated
Dusk, with little respite, transcends into total darkness
Hoping for just a few minutes that silence will prevail
An uneasy calm, lost against a backdrop of complete insanity
Where the wicked and foolish have descended for their amusement
Eating, singing and then sleeping in the place that they now firmly stand
Happy perhaps, blessed of course, naturally uninformed of any other world
Just another day on their path to no place in particular

Beardy

She calls him Beardy
He walks from street to street
She says she hates him
Doesn't know him at all
She stares quite often
He just ignores her
She asks too many questions
Beardy just moves on and on

He is a loner
She makes a point of pointing him out
He makes his bed in the gutter
Begging for a morsel or two
He has no friends
She just can't imagine that
He wants eternal peace
Beardy is defiant in his cause

There are no similarities
One who has and one who has not
Giving up a life in search of a resolution
Living a life in search of a solution
Building a seemingly impossible bridge
Connection to an uncertain future
Co-habiting with a distinct divide
Beardy, the absolute loser

Carlos

Strumming his axe, just like Carlos
Wearing his hat, just like Carlos
Hair, long and curly, just like Carlos
Head tilted, just like Carlos
Voice, full throttle, unlike anything Carlos would sing

Standing alone on a soap box, very alone
Putting his soul into, what was once, soulful music
Bleating like the lamb he has become
Hoping for an audience
Scaring even the kids who laugh in his face

The hardest way to make his ambition come to life
Caught at a cross roads, traffic loud and clear
Drowning his sorrows against a backdrop of blaring horns
Not his ideal wind accompaniment
A shambles on a fine summers evening, for most

His demeanor, changing with each donation
His smile, a never-ending sign of misery
His backup singers, elevated, though invisible
His rhythm, like an electric current gone wrong
His dream, to be just like Carlos, never to be realized

Central Park

I walk, one foot running, towards incarceration
Thinking, watching, curious
Never empty when it comes to ideas
Pondering also a nagging doubt
Filled by noise, coming from near and far, continual noise

Washing their streets, blasting precious resource into oblivion
Cleanliness achieved, but for how long?
Flooding drains with last night's garbage
Dissolving an unmistakable stench of urine, temporarily
Unwilling to give ground to passers by

Then, from the corner of an outstretched arm, food
Food, so much and so frequent
Placed at intervals to suit convenience
Magnificent in presentation, disgusting in abundance
Making it hard to believe that starvation could possibly exist

Greenery, suddenly close and pleasing, Central Park
An oasis perhaps, set amongst never ending dread
Popping up in the unlikeliest of places
Shared by many millions, although never at one time
Spoilt only by the concrete of man's continual folly

And so with much hope in heart, serenity beckons
Paths, to nowhere in particular, offering solace and false impression
Treading carefully amongst remnants of ageing disappointments
Careful not to step on what has become a disgrace
Waking the dead from yet another restless night of living

An exit, ceased in moments, leading to similarity
Bringing, so I thought, an end to misery
Realizing quickly that this had been the starting line
No finish in sight, no medals to give, just one more bagel
Buttered on both sides, but only for the correct gratuity

Dumpsters, shuttling noisily backwards through yesterday's treats
Followed closely by a posse of sadness
Tears flowing endlessly from eyes that rarely shut
Looking for more than just the occasional aluminum can
Feeling scorned by workers content to spin irrelevant jibes

And so, these final strides cover those last few endless yards
Safety found behind doors that have to be locked
Looking once more out into a wilderness that has become a jungle
Finding so few words to describe raging emotion
Asking only, how could we have done this?

Freeway Fred

Walking slowly up the wrong side to nowhere
Pushing tomorrow's meal in a cart from yesteryear
Staggering across debris and oncoming traffic
Oblivious to anyone and anything
Covered in dirt, picked up from his service to cleanliness
Freeway Fed, on a mission to get fed

One or two gentle slopes stand in his way
Completion of an incredulous task, his goal
Sideways glances as money arrives on his busy horizon
Collected with such glee, deposited with affection
Cashing in on a disturbing trend
One man crusade to redeem humanity

A quick breather and then an onslaught
Covering another mile before darkness hides his plight
Side to side, that alcoholic swagger resumes
Determination flashing across his reddened face
Smiling each time he arrives at five cents
Prayers answered just before drink time

Fred fumbles his load then vanishes
Tumbling down that slippery slope to drunkenness
Cashing in, his only aim, as winters chill takes hold
Running with glee towards a recycling heaven
Counting in his head, only unopened bottles
Soon to be empties and then collected by yet another Fred

CPSIA information can be obtained
at www.ICGtesting.com
Printed in the USA
LVHW030043040522
717733LV00014B/505